CONCERNING THE DISCIPLES

CONCERNING THE DISCIPLES

A Brief Resume of the Movement to Restore the New
Testament Church

by

P. H. WELSHIMER

The Standard Publishing Company

CINCINNATI

Printed in U. S. A.

CONTENTS

CONTENTS

TO BEGIN WITH

CHAPTER I

TO BEGIN WITH

It is the purpose of this work to set forth the facts about the "Restoration Movement."

This movement is commonly known under such names as "Christian Church," "Church of Christ," or "Disciples of Christ."

SOME RESTORATION PRINCIPLES

As a people we have no creed but Christ, no book but the Bible. Our plea is the unity of all believers in Christ.

Our program is the restoration of the church of the New Testament in creed, doctrine, polity and life.

Our purpose is the evangelization of the world. It is not now, nor ever has been, our purpose to establish another sect or create another denomination. There are already too many of these.

THE APOSTOLIC CHURCH

"In unity there is strength." The church was united in the beginning, and remained so for a period beyond the first century. "Holy men of God spake as they were moved by the Holy Spirit." Inspired voices never contradict; and so long as their voices were dominant and their unadulterated teaching accepted, only unity could obtain. It was not until after the death of the apostles that error crept in and the apostasy was on the way.

If we can ascertain the nature of the church which had its beginning on Pentecost, as described in Acts, second chapter; if we can know its creed, its doctrine, its polity, its manner of life, then it will be possible to reproduce that church among men today. Can any man hope to improve upon that which is the result of the Holy Spirit's teaching? God was not trying an experiment, Christ was not mistaken in His building, and the apostles were not misled by the Holy Spirit when they carried out a program completely in accord with the Great Commission. The church of today should in every way correspond to the church of the first century in all essential matters.

There was not unity in the apostolic church in nonessentials—matters of mere expediency—but there was unity in the essentials. Our slogan today is, "In essentials, unity; in nonessentials, liberty; in all things, love." We have the right to our opinions about things of which the Lord has not spoken—the type of architecture, the kind of music, the number of instruments to be used, if any, the method of doing our missionary work, the number of services to be held in a day, the length of a sermon, the style of clothing to be worn, and a hundred other things that are matters of mere expediency. They are not essentials to salvation. In these we have the right to an opinion, and the majority should rule. But in such matters as the divinity of Christ, the inspiration of the Scriptures, the Christian ordinances, the name to be worn, the new birth, tests of faith, and all other things actually essentials to the Christian life, we have no opinion, for we need none. Here the Scriptures speak, and "Where the Scriptures speak, we speak; where they are silent, we are silent."

THE NEW TESTAMENT CHURCH

CHAPTER II

THE NEW TESTAMENT CHURCH

Jesus said, "On this rock I will build my church" (Matt. 16: 18). The church began in Jerusalem on the first Pentecost after the resurrection of Jesus the Christ. Jesus told the disciples to tarry in Jerusalem until endued with power from on high. This power came on Pentecost. Referring to this in Acts 11: 15, Peter calls this Pentecost the beginning.

ITS CREED

This church has Christ as its creed (Matt. 16: 16), and this creed is unchangeable (Heb. 13: 8).

ITS NOMENCLATURE

The organization is called:
Church of God (Acts 20: 28).
Church of the Living God (1 Tim. 3: 15).
The Body of Christ (Col. 1: 24).
The Church of Christ (Rom. 16: 16).
The members are called:
Disciples, meaning learners (Acts 11: 26).
Saints, as pertaining to character (Rom. 1: 7).
Brethren, explaining the relationship one to another (1 Cor. 15: 6).
Christians, indicating the relationship to Christ (Acts 11: 26).
Children of the heavenly Father (Gal. 3: 26).

ITS ORDINANCES

The church has two ordinances—Christian baptism and the Lord's Supper.

CONCERNING THE DISCIPLES

Baptism, in the New Testament church, is the burial in water of a penitent believer, in the name of Jesus Christ, for the remission of sins. Infant baptism and sprinkling and pouring are unknown to the New Testament church. The Great Commission (Matt. 28: 18-20), Peter's instruction in Acts 2: 38, Paul's comments in Rom. 6: 4 and Col. 2: 12, and Peter's statement in 1 Pet. 3: 21, make it very clear that baptism is immersion, is intended for penitent believers, is for the remission of sins and the induction into Jesus Christ and His body—the church of Christ.

The Lord's Supper was instituted by Christ Himself, as a memorial. This institution's purpose is to aid the disciples to remember Christ in His death. It points back to His death and forward to His coming, and is to be observed as long as the church remains upon the earth. It is a simple, beautiful memorial, the story of which is recorded in Matt. 26: 26-28. It was observed in the early church upon the first day of every week (Acts 20: 7; 1 Cor. 11: 28).

Its Organization

The organization of the New Testament church consists of membership, elders and deacons. The elders look after the spiritual welfare of the church, and the deacons after the business interests. 1 Tim. 3: 1-13 sets forth the duties and qualifications of elders and deacons. The early church also had preachers and evangelists who were proclaimers of the gospel. The apostles were preachers and evangelists, but the apostolic office ceased with the death of the apostles. The office and work of the preacher and evangelist extend through the Christian dispensation.

Its Doctrine

The New Testament church accepted the Word of God to be its only rule of faith and practice.

Its Unity

The word "church" occurs 114 times in the New Testament. In eighty-five cases out of the 114 the word means a local assembly of

8

Christians—a congregation of believers. In eighteen other cases it refers to the church in general, or "church universal."

There was no great external ecclesiastical organization in the first century, but there was a unity to be found among all the congregations of believers. The churches in all cities and countries were in full agreement on the essential things of the gospel. They wore the same name, had the same creed, observed the same ordinances in the same way and received people into membership in exactly the same manner. All people were received into the church by

Faith in Jesus Christ,
Repentance of their sins,
Confessing Christ before men, and
Being buried with Christ in Christian baptism.

Every revival meeting held and every individual who came into the church observed those steps. They are logical, psychological, fundamental and universal.

That unity of the early churches obtained through all the first century and on through the years until the apostasy, by which we mean the gradual drawing away from the church of the New Testament pattern. Many forces and factors entered into this withdrawal. It was not done in a day, but through the process of years.

It will be well to keep in mind the above facts in the study of the story of the Restoration movement.

THE APOSTASY

CHAPTER III

THE APOSTASY

It is essential to understand the background extending from Pentecost up through the centuries until we reach the beginning of the nineteenth century, to fully appreciate the plea, the plan and the purpose of the church of Christ. In the chapter preceding this, we considered the church as it was in the days of the apostles, as described in doctrine, polity and life, in the New Testament. Had that church continued through the centuries as it began, Christian unity would obtain today, and there would be no such things as Catholicism and denominationalism.

EXTERNAL INFLUENCES

In the second century after the death of all the apostles, and when men who had known the apostles passed to their reward, the trend was slowly and surely away from the church as established under apostolic direction. The apostasy did not come in a day, nor a year, but through the march of the years. Volumes would be required to tell the story completely. Here we can only hint at what took place. Many subtle influences were at work. Monarchial ideas, Greek culture, Oriental mysticism, paganistic philosophy, and ambitious power to rule united in turning the streams of pure doctrine and organization out of their original channels. "Externally, the church preserved its unity—a unity of blood and iron, of chains and absolutism." But this unity was far away from the goal of Jesus and the apostles.

THE RISE OF HIERARCHY

In the New Testament church, elders (also known as bishops, overseers of the flock) directed the church in its spiritnal aspects; but a change came in time, when one of the elders or bishops became the leader in the local church and was especially designated as *the bishop* of the church. Later, over a given group of churches one of these bishops was given authority, and thus this authority grew, until finally, in the year 533, the Emperor Justinian conferred the title, "Lord of the whole church" on the bishop of Rome. Thus began papal domination and thus ended religious liberty. This centralized power sounded the death blow to democracy in the church. The bishop later came to be recognized as "the pope, the vicar of Christ, the successor of the apostle Peter." Here the church was poured into a mold that continued almost unquestioned for a thousand years. All one need do today is to take the body of teaching and the organization of the apostate church as we now find it on earth and lay it down beside the simplicity in organization and doctrine of the New Testament church to see how far away that organization has wandered from the original, and how unlike that church it is in all major respects.

The church of the apostolic days is represented in Revelation, chapters 11 and 12, by the woman who fled to the wilderness for 1,260 years. This was the period of time when the apostate church was to be in full force, supplanting the church of the New Testament.

CORRUPTION OF DOCTRINE

The corruption of the apostate church became so flagrant and its neglect of the Scriptures so monumental that an attempt was made to reform her, which led to the Reformation, begun under Martin Luther, early in the sixteenth century. Of this we shall speak in the next chapter. During the supremacy of the church that had apostatized the Bible was not read by the people; not even the priests had access to it. They had a modified form of the Scriptures, known as the *breviary*, which contained largely matters of tradition.

The ordinances which in the New Testament church were two in number had been increased to seven. The Lord's Supper, instead of being observed on the first day of each week, was observed at different periods of time, and in place of all the people partaking of the loaf, representing the body of Christ, and the cup, representing His blood, the priest, then, and now, is seen partaking of the wine, and the people of the loaf. Baptism, which was immersion, accord-

14

ing to New Testament teaching, was changed through the power of the Roman Catholic Church, and the sprinkling of water upon the individual was substituted for the burial in and resurrection from the water. Many of the customs and doctrines now practiced among numerous Protestant bodies, which are foreign to the New Testament teaching, have been inherited from the Roman Catholic Church, which gradually fell away from the New Testament model.

PREPARATORY TO THE REFORMATION

CHAPTER IV

PREPARATORY TO THE REFORMATION

The period following the development of the apostate church for a thousand years is known in history as the Dark Ages. It includes that desolate and chaotic period from about A. D. 400 to A. D. 1400.

The Rise of Rome

With the growth of the churches in the great cities, preachers were sent into the adjacent country, where churches were organized, which came under the authority of the city church and her bishop, or ruling elder. In time the churches of a given territory constituted a large ecclesiastical body, and from this body the chief bishop, who resided in the city, was called to preside. They called these bodies councils or synods. Through these synods changes were rapidly made, which were a glaring departure from the simplicity of the church of the New Testament. The liberty of the church was curtailed and the power of the bishops increased. In the beginning, these bishops claimed to be delegates of their respective churches, but this delegated group ultimately swung into full power and formed an ecclesiasticism of the most dominant type. The metropolitan city, or maternal city, of a given territory furnished the outstanding bishop or ruler. Rome was the maternal city of the church of Italy, and her bishop was invested with important rites. There were six of these high dignitaries in the six metropolitan cities—Rome, Antioch, Jerusalem, Alexandria, Ephesus and Corinth—but there could not be six heads to one body; hence, an office was created and known as patriarchate—four officers from Rome, Alexandria, Constantinople and Antioch—came into being. These patriarchs consecrated all bishops and had supervision over spiritual matters, and had representatives at foreign courts.

CONCERNING THE DISCIPLES

After the destruction of Jerusalem the church at Rome made claim, although not justified, to be the oldest apostolic church. It also put in its claim for supremacy. Leo (440-451) pressed these claims and is ofttimes called the first of the popes, although it was not until 533 that the Emperor Justinian conferred the title, "Lord of the whole church" on the bishop of Rome. The Eastern patriarchs never acknowledged the supremacy of Rome. In 484 occurred the Great Schism separating the Eastern (Greek Catholic) and the Western (Roman Catholic) churches.

GOD'S FAITHFUL REMNANT

Through all the years God still had a people bearing witness for Him. Everybody was not in accord with this idea of Roman supremacy and the development of the Roman and Greek Catholic Churches. The persecutions, beginning in the second century and continuing on through the third and fourth, drove some of "the faithful" from their homes in Italy to the desolate regions of the Alps. Through the years the teachings and practices of the New Testament were handed down from father to son, and from generation to generation. These people were protected in the Alps when the Gothic nations descended upon Italy, as those nations took another route and left them undisturbed. These people are called Vallenses. They made the claim of having always maintained the simplicity of the gospel of Christ and His apostles.

In 1170, with the coming of Peter Waldo the rich merchant of Lyons, a new impulse was given to these people. He resolved to distribute his wealth among the poor and devote himself to the spreading of the gospel. He had the Scriptures translated into the language of the people. He denounced the Roman Church, calling it the *Babylon of the Apocalypse*. He organized a special order of preachers and missionaries under the title, "The Poor Men of Lyons," who were sent forth, like the early church, to proclaim the gospel of Jesus Christ.

Turning back to the seventh century, we find a man by the name of Constantine of Armenia, who entertained in his home one night a deacon who was returning from captivity in Syria. He presented to him the four Gospels and the fourteen Epistles of Paul.

They revolutionized Constantine's life. He shared his knowledge with his neighbors. A church was founded, much after the principle of the Reformation and the membership was called Paulicians, after the apostle Paul. Later they received the Acts of the Apostles, and the Epistles of James and Jude, and the three Epistles of John. They, too, renounced and denounced all Roman Catholic teaching that was not in harmony with the New Testament Scriptures. They aroused the fury of Rome. A bloody persecution was inaugurated against them. Many of the Paulicians fled about A. D. 755, passing into Thrace and Bulgaria. And here they found the persecutions from Constantinople as furious as those from which they fled. Some remained, but others pressed into Germany, Italy and France. While many names were given them, the most prominent was Cathari, or Puritans. They settled about the city of Albi, and hence received the name of Albigenses. Rome attempted their destruction in the early part of the eleventh century. A remnant fled to the Alps and took refuge with the Vallenses. From this time on the Albigenses seemed to lose their identity and they were gradually absorbed by the Vallenses. Their faith was the same and their persecutions similar.

Thus we see there was a spark of the old faith and an adherence to the scriptural teaching remaining on the earth through all those bloody years. The Albigenses were a law-abiding, modest people who dressed simply and lived nobly. On the other hand, the church of Rome, which had departed from the teaching of the New Testament Scriptures, had grown so corrupt that early in the sixteenth century a movement began which, while called the Reformation, reformed nothing, but ended in a withdrawal from the apostate church and was the beginning of Protestantism.

Concerning this we shall give attention in the next chapter. All of this study is essential for the background and a real understanding of the Restoration movement of the nineteenth century, to which we shall give much attention in future chapters.

THE REFORMATION

CHAPTER V

THE REFORMATION

We have seen in our former study that the organization and doctrine of the New Testament church were quite simple. In organization it functioned perfectly. Its doctrine was essential. One has but to study the New Testament Scriptures to see the high moral plane on which it stood.

In the Middle Ages, along with the decline in organization and doctrine, the decline in morals was very noticeable.

The Lutheran Movement

The Reformation was motivated more by the attempt to purify the church in morals than to rectify its doctrinal position. When Martin Luther visited Rome and saw the scandalous behavior of the clergy he was thoroughly aroused. Later this German monk, who was a priest, opposed Pope Leo who favored Tetzel (1515) in preaching his doctrine of indulgences to raise money to help build Saint Peter's Cathedral. Aroused by this inconsistency Martin Luther nailed his ninety-five theses to the doors of Wittenberg Cathedral. The echo of that hammer was heard around the world. It meant a break forever with the Church of Rome.

Luther found a copy of the Bible chained to a bookstall in his monastery, and reading it he became the promulgator of the doctrine of justification by faith. Up to this time the people were ignorant of biblical teaching. The priests had a modified form of the Bible known as the *breviary*, which contained a mixture of biblical teaching and traditions. Now Luther came to the conclusion that the Bible was God's Book for the people and should be *read* by them rather than be *interpreted* by the priests. He translated the Scriptures into the German vernacular and the people were enabled to read the Bible in their own tongue. It was easy for them to see the difference

3

between the church described in the New Testament and the one then in existence.

Other reformers playing a conspicious part in the breaking away from the Church of Rome were Zwingli, Calvin, Lattimer, Huss, John Knox, Savonarola and others. John Calvin played a great part in the Reformation. He was born in 1509 and received his education in the Universities of Orleans and Paris preparing for law, but later turned to theology. He stressed the divine sovereignty of God.

THE REFORMATION IN ENGLAND

The Reformation in England was semipolitical. While it partook of the essential characteristics of Protestantism it clung to much that had been inherited from Roman Catholicism. While there was a revolution in theology and doctrine, there was still the inheritance of the hierarchy stressing unity of church and state. The Anglican Church claims to be neither Catholic nor Protestant and endeavors to occupy the middle ground hoping to unite the Protestant and Catholic bodies, a thing which can never be done on any basis except that of the New Testament Scriptures.

Out of this movement in England came many independent movements, the most notable of which was the Puritan movement led by Oliver Cromwell. This had great influence in America. The English Reformation left England with the Anglican Church, Scotland with the Presbyterian, and failing to win Ireland, left it strongly Roman Catholic.

THE WESLEYAN MOVEMENT

John Wesley was born at Epworth in 1703. His father was a clergyman of the Church of England. John Wesley and his brother Charles, while in college, began a methodical study of the Bible. They revolted against the formalism of the English church. In reality, Methodism was a movement within a movement, there being no attempt to organize a new church, but, rather, an attempt to spiritualize the Episcopal Church. But it was impossible to put new wine in old bottles. While Wesley died in the communion of the Anglican Church, and was buried in the surplice of that church, out of the spirit of his teaching came the great body known today as the Methodist Church.

So in the study of all denominations we find they have been built around one commanding principle or article of faith. They began by stressing something which others had neglected to stress. The founding of each was an attempt either to purify the existing church, or to stress a doctrine not hitherto prominently taught, until today we have scores of denominations possessing common doctrines and furnishing little evidence to the world of the necessity of their separate existence.

THE SETTING FOR THE RESTORATION

CHAPTER VI

THE SETTING FOR THE RESTORATION

We have, up to this point, been studying conditions which existed in Europe. With the discovery and settlement of the New World practically all of the varied religious bodies in Europe were planted here and our religious problems became almost identical to those in the mother country.

MORAL AND SOCIAL CONDITIONS

The moral and spiritual conditions of the people of the United States one hundred and thirty years ago were extremely low. Unbelief was prevalent. The dark pall of infidelity had settled over the nation. Religion was blamed for many of the evils from which men suffered. During the Revolutionary War infidel France had sown the seeds of infidelity in this country.

The aftermath of the Revolutionary War was upon the country and the tendency of war is to lower the moral tone of the people engaged in it. The people in the United States were exceedingly poor. They were widely separated from each other. At the close of the Revolutionary War many of the people were practically anarchists. They desired liberty so greatly that it merged into license and they were against almost any kind of government.

The moral life of the people was on a low plane. Slavery existed without rebuke. Gentlemen settled their difficulties by fighting duels. Intoxication was rampant. There were no organizations agitating temperance or total abstinence. Members of churches drank to intoxication and ministers were frequently paid their salaries in liquor. The Lord's Day was desecrated.

The Bible was an unknown book to most of the people. During the time that King George ruled over the Thirteen Colonies an edict was issued forbidding the Bible to be printed on Colonial soil.

CONCERNING THE DISCIPLES

RELIGIOUS CONDITIONS

Many of those who did believe in God, in the Christ and in the Bible, were Calvinistic. They held that a definite number of men were foreordained to everlasting life, irrespective of belief or conduct. With this belief there was nothing for a man to do to secure his salvation. Parents objected to preachers speaking to their sons and daughters on the subject of personal religion. Revival meetings were not held. What was the use? If it were already determined that men were saved or lost, why preach to them? Faith was considered a direct gift from God, and therefore it was useless to preach the gospel to produce faith. Bible schools, missionary societies and tract societies were supposed to exist contrary to the will of God. People who were identified with these movements were considered heretics.

In that far away day human creeds had a power over people. They were rigid tests of fellowship. One had to subscribe to them in order to get into the church. To renounce one of those creeds was the same in the mind of the people as renouncing religion. The creeds were unchangeable and final.

The office of the clergy had been greatly magnified. It was believed by the common people that no one understood the Bible but the clergy. And woe be to that layman who controverted the teaching of the clergy. The ordinances of baptism and the Lord's Supper were administerd only by the clergy.

The Bible as taught was largely the cause of confusion. The different dispensations—Patriarchal, Jewish and Christian—were confused. The Word of Truth was not rightly divided. The rules which applied to the study of other literature were not applied to Bible study.

The Westminster Confession of Faith set forth the doctrine of total depravity. The unconverted did not seek God, but were passive, waiting for God to seek them. They were as helpless as a dead man bound in grave clothes, and only the voice of God could bid them come forth. Evangelistic meetings were few. Evangelism was almost dead. The whole matter of saving people was in the hands of God. Preaching was of but little use and had but little effect upon the people. Every conversion was an extraordinary act. The people were taught to accept dreams, see strange lights, hear unusual sounds, see visions, have peculiar feelings, and, sad to say, this teaching has not been entirely eliminated from the minds of men. The emotional were reached, while sane men who thought this through, were untouched and were led into skepticism. Others, not receiving these signs nor experiencing the feelings, considered themselves among the lost. What a situation! The Bible was a dead letter in place of the Living Word.

Christians were divided into warring camps. The unity that obtained in the first century was unknown. Preachers of one church never appeared in the pulpit of another. The religious controversies were productive of discord; "the peace that passeth understanding" was absent. Then, as now, many communities were overchurched and unable to employ capable men—merely eked out an existence. Money was wasted, talent undeveloped, the strength that comes through union was absent, and the churches constituted a warring camp.

A MOVEMENT FOR THE TIMES

These were some of the conditions prevailing when Thomas Campbell came to America from Ireland, near the beginning of the nineteenth century. With this background one is prepared better to understand the origin of the Restoration movement and the plea for the unity of all believers in Christ.

The time had come to rekindle the fire on the altars of Jehovah. God always has His leaders at the proper time. There was a time for Moses to lead Israel from Egypt. Esther delivered the Jews at the proper hour. The Reformers came in the fullness of time. The work done by Luther, Calvin, Wesley, and many others was essential to the beginning of the still greater movement to restore the church as it was in the days of the apostles.

The Restoration leaders accepted all the good and all that was scriptural which had been stressed by the Reformers, and, standing upon their shoulders, saw further than did the Reformers. They took as their rule of faith and practice the Word of God alone. They accepted Christ as Lord, the divine Son of God, to whom had been given all authority. With the lordship of Jesus and His authoritative Word they began the movement which is destined to bring about the answer to the prayer of Jesus, "that they all may

33

be one." They showed a difference between the Old Testament and the New Testament. The entire Book is from God, but it consists of two Testaments. The law was for the Jewish people for a limited time, the gospel is for all peoples for all time. "The Old Testament is the New concealed; the New is the Old revealed." It placed before the world Jesus Christ as "the creed that needs no revision." They called Bible things by Bible names. They placed the ordinances in their proper place. They showed that Christian baptism set forth the death, burial and resurrection of Jesus, the last step one takes in coming into the kingdom of God, the meeting of the Christ where He has promised to meet us. They taught, and rightly so, that the Holy Spirit was "not a command to be preached, but a promise to be enjoyed." The Holy Spirit is God's side of the matter of salvation. It is ours to obey, while it is God's prerogative to grant the promised results when one has rendered obedience. They presented the great facts of the gospel which created faith, and took as their slogan, "Where the Scriptures speak, we speak; and where they are silent, we are silent." Opinions were not at warfare with faith. Opinions were not permitted to be a test of fellowship. Opinions were exercised only where the Book does not speak. They preached Jesus Christ a person, not a system of doctrine. The pre-eminence of the Christ overshadowed all else.

THE MOVEMENT'S BEGINNING AND PURPOSE

CHAPTER VII

THE MOVEMENT'S BEGINNING AND PURPOSE

Thomas and Alexander Campbell, father and son, were not founders of the Christian Church. They were preachers, who, with others at the beginning of the nineteenth century, became dissatisfied with the divided condition of Christendom and set themselves to the task of restoring the church as it was in the days of the apostles. They were restorers and not reformers. They were preachers and not founders of the church.

THE PLACE OF THE CAMPBELLS

The Campbells were leaders in the Restoration movement, and because of that fact some have misunderstood their labors and called them builders or founders of the church, and their followers were sometimes nicknamed "Campbellites." A "Campbellite" would be a follower of Thomas and Alexander Campbell. Paul condemned this idea of following men, in his first Corinthian Epistle (1 Cor. 1: 10-15). We were not baptized into the Campbells, but were baptized into the Christ and therefore bear His name and follow Him. We honor the Campbells and their colaborers because of their initiative, their vision and their ability to search the Scriptures and lead the bewildered, confused religious world back to the Christ and the church established by His authority in Jerusalem on the first Pentecost after His resurrection and ascension.

THE PURPOSE OF THE CAMPBELLS

The men of that day were already too tired and sick of a divided Christendom to think of adding another denomination to the already existing number. Their purpose was to heal the divisions, unite the people into one body, the church of Christ. To do this they went back of the creeds of Augsburg, Westminster, Nicea and Rome, back to Jerusalem and to Antioch, to the teaching as found in the Scriptures written in the first century. They did not undervalue the faith of the followers of Christ in their day but they did see the mistakes which many followers were making, and simply laid before them the Bible and said, "Follow the Scriptures and you will be following Christ." There was nothing narrow about that position. There is nothing narrow about it today. It is the thing which the religious world today desires. A divided church is not in accord with the New Testament position and a divided church can not save the world.

OTHERS OF LIKE MIND

The Campbells were Presbyterians at the beginning of the Restoration movement. There were others who desired to get back to the simplicity of New Testament teaching and practice. James O'Kelly was a Methodist. He became dissatisfied with the existing order of things, and especially with the prevailing Episcopal form of government. On Christmas day, 1763, at Manakin Town, N. C., he established a congregation, taking the New Testament as its only discipline and rule of faith and practice. They called themselves Christians. In 1800 Dr. Abner Jones, a Baptist preacher, established congregations at Lyndon, Vt., and Bradford and Pierpont, N. H., which wore no name but Christian, and took the Bible as their rule of faith and practice. These movements, antedating that of the Campbells, reveal the fact that there was everywhere a deep, spiritual urge in the hearts of men of all creeds for a return to the New Testament order.

THOMAS CAMPBELL

CHAPTER VIII

THOMAS CAMPBELL.

The name of Thomas Campbell stands prominently among the leaders of the Restoration movement. Eclipsed in later years by his son, Alexander, it must be remembered that father laid the foundation on which the son built. They were not rivals, but were colaborers in a common cause.

ANCESTRY

Thomas Campbell was born in County Down, Ireland, Feb. 1, 1763. He was well-born, his ancestors having come from western Scotland. His grandfather, Thomas Campbell, born in the same county, died at the age of one hundred five. His father, Archibald Campbell, was a British soldier and fought under Wolfe at Quebec. When a young man, Archibald Campbell was a Roman Catholic, but later united with the Church of England.

EARLY MINISTRY

Thomas Campbell was repelled by the formality and stiffness of the Church of England and united with the Seceder Presbyterians. At the age of twenty-four he entered Glasgow University, to prepare for the ministry. Having finished the course, he entered the theological school of the Seceder Presbyterian Church, at Whithouse. Having preached as a "probationer," filling in for congregations that had no regular ministers, at the age of thirty-five we find him located on a farm near Rich Hill, while he preached for the church at Ahorey. He remained with this church nine years. The old stone church in which he preached, 30 x 60 feet, still stands and is used by the congregation as a place of worship.

Mr. Campbell was a strong preacher, popular, well-read, a thorough student of the Scriptures, pious, spiritually-minded and greatly devoted

4

to the cause of Christ. Alexander Campbell, his son, said of him, "I never knew a man of whom it could be said with more assurance that he walked with God."

LATER INFLUENCES

He was distressed by the divisions among God's people. Sectarian bitterness and strife had no place in his make-up. While Barton W. Stone and others in the early years of the nineteenth century, were turning away from sectarianism and organizing churches of the New Testament order, Thomas Campbell was laboring with the people of his own country to eliminate divisions and eradicate the sectarian spirit.

In 1806, Mr. Campbell was sent on a mission to the general synod of Scotland, at Glasgow, where he presented the cause of unity with much fervor, trying to unite the "Burgers" and the "Anti-Burgers," but his message fell upon dull ears. Their petty differences were more to them than the larger welfare of the kingdom of God.

The Campbell home life was most delightful. In June, 1787, he married Miss Jane Corneigle. There were prayers and Bible reading in the family both morning and night. His was a churchgoing family. While preaching at Ahorey he came in contact with the people known as the Independents. He had the privilege of hearing such preachers as Rowland Hill, Robert Haldane, Alexander Carson and John Walker. These people had separated from the Church of England.

EMIGRATION TO AMERICA

Mr. Campbell was not a successful farmer. His salary was small, ranging from $150.00 to $200.00 a year. His family was increasing. He opened a school hoping to add to his usefulness and his income. His physician recommended a long sea voyage as a means of recuperating his health. Alexander, his son, having told him it was his purpose to go to America when of age, and requesting the father to go ahead and select a home, motivated him to America. He also hoped in this land to find more fertile soil for the seed of unity. Apr. 8, 1807, Mr. Campbell bade farewell to his church and family and set sail. Arriving in America, he settled in western Pennsylvania, where he soon obtained employment as a minister in the presbytery of Chartiers, near Pittsburgh.

EARLY AMERICAN MINISTRY

One Sunday morning he invited the members of other communions to partake of the Lord's Supper. This stamped him as being heterodox, and for the offense he was tried before the presbytery to which he belonged, and was found guilty. Note that the charge was that he invited folk of other communions to partake of the Lord's Supper from the same table, in the same house, on the same day. That gives us some idea of the fierceness of the sectarian spirit of that time. Appealing to the associate synod of North America, he made an eloquent defense and the sentence was reversed, and the censure administered by his own presbytery was removed. This, however, produced strained relations between himself and his church. Thomas Campbell wrote "The Declaration and Address" a little later. We shall discuss this more fully in another chapter. He was the author of the slogans now familiar to all of our people—"Where the Bible speaks, we speak; where the Bible is silent, we are silent." It was he who said, "A 'thus saith the Lord' either in expressed terms or by approved precedent for every article of faith and item of religious practice." He said, "Nothing ought to be received into the faith or worship of the church or be made a test of faith among Christians that is not as old as the New Testament." He set forth the plan of union in these words: "The restoration of primitive Christianity in its doctrine, its ordinances and its practices." These were great slogans and are powerful even to this day.

ALEXANDER CAMPBELL

CHAPTER IX

ALEXANDER CAMPBELL

Alexander Campbell was born Sept. 12, 1788, near Shane's castle, County Antrim, Ireland. He was the son of Thomas and Jane Campbell. The mother was a descendant of the French Huguenots, an agricultural people who came from France to Scotland and later to Ireland. They were Presbyterians.

His Boyhood

Alexander Campbell spent his boyhood days on a farm, while his father preached for the church at Ahorey. He first went to primary school at Marken Hill, then to an academy established by his uncles, Archibald and Enos Campbell, at Newry. He then returned home and his father became his teacher, laying the foundation for his liberal education. The boy liked outdoor sports and was not over-fond of study at this period of life. He had a strong body in which to house a great mind. He made a study of the languages, and familiarized himself with the Bible. As a young man he made an extended study of Romanism and its effects upon the people. Episcopalianism was to him a cold, aristocratic religion. Although a Presbyterian, he found that church split up into many divisions and possessing a sectarian spirit not in harmony with his views of Christian religion.

His Education

Alexander Campbell was nineteen years of age when his father set sail for America. If satisfied on this continent the family was to be sent for. The next fall they attempted to join him, but the vessel was wrecked. However, the family was saved. It was at that time that Alexander Campbell formed the resolution that he would give himself wholly to God and spend his life as a minister

47

of His Word. The season being far spent the family decided to remain in Scotland until the next year, which gave the young man the opportunity of taking studies in the University of Glasgow.

Glasgow was a city of 114,000 population. To this young man, coming from the rural and village life, wonderful opportunities presented themselves for study and observation. There were fifteen hundred students enrolled. This was the *alma mater* of his father. Some of his father's teachers were still on the faculty. He stood first in his class in logic, under Professor Jardine, who had been his father's professor. He arose at four in the morning and retired at ten in the evening. With a strong body he was enabled to spend long hours with his books. He stood at the front in his classes, did much general reading, and defrayed most of his expenses in teaching private classes. The Haldanes and their colaborers influenced his religious life while in the university. Here a church of which a Mr. Ewing was pastor had broken away from the custom of observing the Lord's Supper twice a year, and introduced its weekly observance. Some of these leaders were attempting to restore the church in doctrine, polity and life as it was in the first century. Though Mr. Campbell was a member of the Seceder Presbyterian Church, he was tired of denominationalism and was about ready to declare himself for the one body of Christ, as set forth in the New Testameent. There were many things which he desired to discuss with his father when he arrived on American soil. When he walked out of the university, taking his departure for America, one of the professors standing in a group said to the others, "There goes a young man who will some day move the world."

His Arrival in America

His father had landed in Philadelphia, May 27, 1807. Sept. 29, 1809, Alexander Campbell and the other members of the Thomas Campbell family arrived in New York harbor. They spent two days sight-seeing, made a brief stop at Philadelphia and then started on the long overland trip of three hundred and fifty miles across the mountains to Washington, Pa., to meet the father. The father was so anxious to see the family that he started to meet them, and they met on one of the mountains in Pennsylvania, three days away from Washington, Pa. During that three days the father and son discussed the important things which had transpired since their separation, the most important of which was the publication of "The Declaration and Address," to which we shall give attention later. This was the first thing read by Alexander Campbell in America. He said to his father that he proposed to devote his life to the propagation of the principles contained in it. Father and son, separated by the vast ocean, had, through the months, come to the same viewpoint. The influences which had been brought to bear upon the son in the university, and the father in the new land, were certainly of God, and proclaimed His interest in the tasks to which they were committing themselves. The Campbells thought all these steps providential, and who will dare say they were not?

Beginnings of His Ministry

Washington, Pa., was a village of five hundred inhabitants. Here Alexander Campbell began anew the study of the Bible, with the assistance of his father. He did nothing but study the Bible for six months. In his twenty-second year he closed one of his father's meetings with an exhortation, his first attempt at speaking in public. He preached his first sermon the same year—July 15, 1810. The meeting place was a grove near their home where a large audience had assembled. Some who heard, said he was a greater preacher than his father. The text was Matt. 7: 24-27—"Whosoever heareth these sayings of mine, and doeth them, I will liken him to a wise man who built his house on a rock: . . ."

The father and son established a church in the wilderness, known as Brush Run, May 4, 1811, with thirty members. Here Alexander Campbell was ordained a preacher, Jan. 1, 1812. They had before them two ruling principles—the supreme authority of the Scriptures, and the union of the people of God. Other questions which arose later were settled by New Testament teaching. The first meeting was held June 16. Alexander Campbell preached, and the Lord's Supper was observed. Up to this time neither of the Campbells had been immersed. We shall hear much more of Alexander Campbell and how he met and solved some of the problems, in future chapters.

"THE DECLARATION AND ADDRESS"

CHAPTER X

"THE DECLARATION AND ADDRESS"

When Thomas Campbell preached one Sunday morning in the Allegheny Valley to the Seceder Presbyterians, he found present in the audience members of other Presbyterian bodies. As mentioned in a previous chapter, he invited them all to the Lord's Table. At the next meeting of the presbytery he was called to account for this act and publicly censured for his conduct. Mr. Campbell appealed to the synod of North America. That body removed the censure of the lower court, in form, but reaffirmed it in fact by stating that there were sufficient grounds for censure.

BREAK WITH THE PRESBYTERIANS

Thomas Campbell then severed all ministerial connection with the synod of North America. He preached in the homes of his friends, and crowds came to hear him. Aug. 17, 1809, they organized the Christian Association of Washington, Pennsylvania. Twenty-one persons were appointed to recommend the best means of promoting the organization. They erected on the Sinclair farm, three miles from Mt. Pleasant, on the road leading from Washington, Pa., a log building, to be used for school and church purposes. Mr. Campbell lived in the home of a farmer by the name of Welch, near by. In this quiet place he wrote the report for the committee of twenty-one, which was first read to them Sept. 7, 1809, and is known as "THE DECLARATION AND ADDRESS." It contains more than thirty thousand words and was then, and still remains, a great document.

SUMMARY OF THE DECLARATION

"The Declaration and Address" has thirteen points, briefly stated as follows:

53

CONCERNING THE DISCIPLES

1. The church of Christ on earth is essentially, intentionally and constitutionally one consisting of all those in every place that profess Christ and obedience to Him in all things, according to the Scriptures, and that manifest the same by their tempers and conduct.

2. There should be no schisms or uncharitable divisions among congregations of believers. The churches should walk by the same rule and speak the same thing.

3. Nothing should be inculcated as articles of faith nor required as terms of communion but what is expressly taught in the Word of God, either in expressed terms or by approved precedent.

4. The Old and New Testaments make a perfect revelation of the divine will; the New Testament is a perfect constitution for the worship, discipline and government of the New Testament church.

5. Human authority has no power to impose new commands and ordinances not enjoined by the Lord. Nothing ought to be received into the faith or worship of the church or be made a term of communion among Christians, that is not as old as the New Testament.

6. Faith must stand in the power of God, not the wisdom of men. Inferences and deductions from Scripture premises may be truly called the doctrine of God's Word, yet they are not binding upon the consciences of Christians further than they perceive the connection.

7. Doctrinal exhibitions of divine truth ought not to be made terms of Christian communion.

8. Admission into the church is permissible to those who realize their lost condition, recognize the way of salvation through Jesus Christ, confess Him, and render obedience to Him.

9. All that are enabled to make profession and to manifest it in their conduct should consider others in the church as the saints of God and should live together as children of the heavenly Father.

10. Divisions among Christians is a horrid evil. It is anti-Christian and antiscriptural. It destroys the love that should obtain among brethren.

11. A partial neglect of the revealed will of God, an assumed authority for making human opinions and human inventions terms of communion, have proved acknowledged causes of divisions.

12. Those are to be received as members in the church who have due measure of scriptural knowledge and profess their faith in Christ and obedience to Him in all things, according to the Scriptures.

54

They will continue in membership, when by their conduct they continue to manifest the reality of their profession. Nothing is to be considered in the articles of faith and holiness except what is expressly revealed in the Word of God. The ordinances are to be carefully observed after the example of the primitive church exhibited in the New Testament.

13. Human expediences are never to be permitted to produce contentions nor divisions in the church.

THE CAMPBELLS AND BAPTISM

CHAPTER XI

THE CAMPBELLS AND BAPTISM

Thomas and Alexander Campbell were originally members of the Seceder Presbyterian Church and, according to the custom of that church, practiced sprinkling for baptism and administered the same to babies. Like multitudes of others since their day, they had given no special attention to the teaching of the Bible on the subject of baptism.

An Important Principle

But the father and son had now agreed that all religious questions were to be settled by the Bible. Their slogan was, "Where the Bible speaks, we speak; and where the Bible is silent, we are silent." Of necessity, this slogan would lead them far from the path in which they were then walking.

Infant Baptism

Alexander Campbell, at the very beginning of his ministry, preached on Mark 16: 15, 16, and said, "As I am sure it is unscriptural to make this matter a term of communion I let it slip. I wish to think and let think on these matters." Nearly all the members of that congregation of Brush Run had been sprinkled in infancy and had been taught that the ordinance was a proper induction into the church.

Alexander Campbell married Miss Margaret Brown, the daughter of John Brown, of Brook County, W. Va., March 13, 1811. A year later a girl was born into their home. At once the question of baptizing the baby came to the front. Being a thorough Greek scholar, the father began a careful investigation as to the teaching of the Scriptures upon this subject, and was soon convinced that baptism was for penitent believers and not for babies.

CONCERNING THE DISCIPLES

THE ACTION OF BAPTISM

His investigation also revealed that New Testament baptism was by immersion. It is the burial in and the resurrection from water, of a penitent believer, in the name of Jesus Christ, for the remission of sins.

This being true, Mr. Campbell was convinced that he had not been baptized. His wife agreed with him. He conferred with his father, who was rather reticent on the subject, but, like the son, began to give careful study to the matter. Alexander Campbell's sister Dorothea came to the brother with the startling statement that she, too, had read her Bible carefully and was convinced there was no authority for infant baptism in the Bible.

THE CAMPBELLS IMMERSED

Alexander Campbell conferred with Matthias Luce, a Baptist preacher, and set June 12, 1812, as a day for the baptizing in Buffalo Creek. Mr. Luce and another Baptist preacher, Henry Spears, on his way to the baptizing, spent the night with Thomas Campbell. The next day there appeared at the home of David Bryant, near the Buffalo Creek, a large audience. Thomas Campbell preached a sermon, giving the reasons which had led him to believe that immersion was the New Testament action of baptism. Alexander Campbell followed in an address, emphasizing that immersion alone was biblical baptism, and that only penitent believers were subjects for baptism. James Hanen and wife were convinced by these addresses, so on that day Mr. and Mrs. Thomas Campbell, Mr. and Mrs. Alexander Campbell, and his sister Dorothea, and Mr. and Mrs. James Hanen, seven in all, were baptized by Mr. Luce. Alexander Campbell led Mr. Luce, the Baptist, to agree with him that the ordinance should be in harmony with the New Testament pattern, and as there was no precedent for the "religious experiences" practiced by Baptists as a prerequisite for baptism, this was to be omitted, and the Campbells and others simply made the "Good Confession," made by Peter, that "Jesus is the Christ, the Son of the living God" (Matt. 16: 17, 18). This was a departure from Baptist usage, and was probably the first time on American soil that the "Good Con-

60

fession," as practiced in the church of the New Testament, was so honored.

The next day at the Brush Run Church thirteen others confessed their faith in Christ and were buried in Christian baptism, Thomas Campbell officiating. Others followed and in a short time the church was composed entirely of baptized believers.

THE CAMPBELLS AND THE BAPTISTS

CHAPTER XII

THE CAMPBELLS AND THE BAPTISTS

The organization at Brush Run, having accepted immersion, attracted the attention of the Baptists. There was bitter opposition to the immersionist program by the Presbyterians, who were strong in the community at that time.

AFFILIATION WITH THE BAPTISTS

The Baptists were not numerous in the vicinity of Brush Run. Eastward, on the Monongahela River, and in the valleys at the base of the Allegheny Mountains, they had an association called "Redstone Association," named for an old Indian fort on the river, about sixty miles from Pittsburgh. This Redstone Association invited Brush Run to enter their fellowship. They were glad to accept such scholarly leaders as Thomas and Alexander Campbell. It must be remembered the Campbells were not desirous of forming a new denomination, and upon certain conditions, agreed to enter the Redstone Association. In the autumn of 1813, the Brush Run organization agreed to accept the Baptist invitation, on condition that they be "allowed to teach and preach whatever they learned from the Holy Scriptures, regardless of any creed or formula in Christendom." They were accepted.

DEBATES ON FUNDAMENTALS

The Baptist churches were thrown open to Alexander Campbell and his services were widely sought. He discussed in their meetings the subjects that are today paramount in the Restoration movement; such as baptism—its place and purpose, the Lord's Supper, conversion, Christian union, the two covenants, the law and the gospel. He came to be the recognized leader among those religious forces. In 1820 he debated the baptismal question with John Walker, at Mt.

Pleasant, O., and in 1822, he debated the same question with William McCalla, at Washington, Ky. Mr. Campbell said, "A week's debating is worth a year's preaching." In 1816, Mr. Campbell preached his famous "Sermon on the Law," at a meeting of the Redstone Association, at Cross Creek, Va. This sermon was the entering wedge which led to the separation between Mr. Campbell and the Baptists. This was an epoch-making sermon, setting forth the distinction between the law and the gospel. The sermon led to a heresy trial, but he was acquitted. The Brush Run church withdrew from the Redstone Association and united with the Mahoning Baptist Association of eastern Ohio, in 1823. Mr. Campbell and thirty others, mostly of Brush Run, organized the church at Wellsburg, Va., the same year.

"THE CHRISTIAN BAPTIST" LAUNCHED

The Christian Baptist was launched to espouse the cause of no religious sect except that ancient sect "called Christians first at Antioch." Mr. Campbell erected a building near his home, bought presses and type, and pushed this enterprise vigorously. To mail the paper a post office was established in his home and was called Bethany—"house of bread." For the next thirty years Mr. Campbell was the postmaster. The first issue of *The Christian Baptist* came from the press July 4, 1823, and in 1830 it ceased to exist, giving place to *The Millennial Harbinger*, a monthly paper double the size of the *Baptist*. The writings of Mr. Campbell stirred the people of all religious bodies. They created discussions. Some were with him and many were against him. There was a general religious upheaval. People were shaken out of the old ruts, old forms and molds were broken and they were given to understand religion in the clear light of New Testament teaching. The clergy, which had misled the people so long, were characterized as "hireling priests," "textuary divines," and "scrap doctors." They were scored for "clerical dress," "sanctimonious speech," "long-faced piety," and for wearing the title of "Reverend," "Bishop," "Doctor," etc. Several associations which had been exercising legislative and judiciary authority gave up their organizations and became simply annual meetings for counsel and fellowship.

THE CAMPBELLS AND THE BAPTISTS

THE BAPTIST CREED

At that time creeds had a strong grip on the people. The "Philadelphia Confession" was popular among the Baptists. Any one ignoring it could have no fellowship among them. At a meeting of the Redstone Association in 1827, which was attended by Mr. Campbell as a corresponding messenger from the Mahoning Association, fourteen congregations were refused admittance because their representatives failed to declare allegiance to the Philadelphia Confession. Mr. Campbell denounced this procedure, declaring that in opinions people should be free, and he held the Philadelphia Confession to be nothing more than the opinions of men. He wrote a series of editorials called "The Ancient Order of Things," covering the apostolic faith and practice. The friends of Mr. Campbell were stigmatized as "Restorationers" and "Campbellites." All kinds of accusations were brought against him, some going so far as to call him a Unitarian.

CHAPTER XIII

WITHDRAWAL FROM THE BAPTIST CHURCH

Thomas and Alexander Campbell were unsectarian and were set against denominational divisions. They had affiliated with the Baptist Church, with the understanding that freedom was to be granted in proclaiming New Testament doctrines as they understood them. They were still somewhat hazy as to the complete plan of the Restoration movement. This, with their aversion to divisions, accounts for fellowship with the Baptist Church.

The publication of *The Christian Baptist* gave Alexander Campbell a great audience. His influence increased as his work became more extended. Co-operating with him in Kentucky were such men as P. S. Fall, "Raccoon" John Smith, John T. Johnson and others, who were Baptists but later left the Baptist fold. In Ohio were such leaders as Adamson Bently, Walter Scott, Joseph Gaston and William Hayden.

PREACHING THE "ANCIENT ORDER"

Walter Scott was employed as evangelist for the Mahoning Association in 1827. The Association was composed of Baptist churches in eastern Ohio, between the Ohio River on the east and Lake Erie, and was known as the Western Reserve. Walter Scott, only thirty years of age, was a great evangelist and a close friend and admirer of Alexander Campbell. He was a student of the Bible and ventured forth boldly to preach the gospel as it was preached in apostolic days. He was preaching at a time when Calvinism and infidelity were bitter opponents to his message. The first year under his evangelism, there were one thousand conversions in the Western Reserve. He stood for the "ancient order of things." Many Baptist churches dropped the Philadelphia Confession and accepted the New Testament in its place. The Deerfield Methodist Church joined the movement as a whole. Thomas Campbell visited Walter Scott at New Lisbon, Apr. 9, 1828. He wrote to his son, Alexander Campbell, commending the work of Walter Scott, in his proclaiming the ancient gospel. He was pleased with Scott's application of the gospel. This evangelistic spirit spread over Kentucky, Ohio, western Pennsylvania, Illinois, Indiana, Missouri, Tennessee and Virginia. Much of this can be attributed to the influence of *The Christian Baptist*.

OPPOSITION TO OLD-LINE BAPTISTS

The enemies of Mr. Campbell were active. There was no small tempest among Baptist preachers and congregations, as all were not in accord with the Campbellian movement. The Campbells hoped that the Baptist Church would return completely to apostolic ground. Mr. Campbell said, "I am for peace, for union, for harmony, for co-operation with all men." The separation from the Baptist Church finally came. The Campbells and their colaborers were forced into a separate communion.

POINTS OF DISAGREEMENT

The cause of separation was both doctrinal and practical. The two bodies disagreed on *the proper division of the Bible*. As a people we do not discard, nor have we ever discarded the Old Testament, except "the handwriting of ordinances that was against us, which was contrary to us," and which was by Christ taken out of the way, "nailing it to his cross." (Col. 2: 14.) While both books are accepted, the Old Testament was for the Jew, the New Testament for the Christian dispensation. The moral principles of the Old Testament are immortal. "The Old Testament is the New Testament concealed, while the New Testament is the Old Testament revealed." But the Baptists insisted upon the equal authority of both books in the life of the Christian.

They disagreed upon *the design of baptism*. The New Testament teaches that baptism is connected with the remission of sins. Obedience in baptism brings about the change of state, and with it the forgiveness of sins. The Baptists taught that baptism was to be administered because sins had already been remitted.

They differed on *the question of conversion*. The Baptists were Calvinistic and taught that man was dead in trespasses and in sins, and that nothing save a spiritual miracle, through the direct operation of the Holy Spirit could give him spiritual life. The Campbells held that men were taught to believe, and through faith were led to repentance and accepted Christ of their own volition.

They disagreed on *creeds*. The Baptists favored statements of doctrinal belief, most of them having adopted the Philadelphia Confession. The Campbells insisted that Bible things should be stated in Bible terms and that creeds were a prolific source of division. They taught that Christ is the creed, and the Word of God is the rule of faith and practice.

The Baptists taught that only an ordained preacher had *the right to baptize*. The Campbells taught that any Christian had the right to administer the ordinances of the Lord.

The Baptists observed the *Lord's Supper* once a month, or once a quarter, while Mr. Campbell insisted that according to New Testament teaching it should be observed every Lord's Day. This was the practice of the primitive church. The Baptists practiced close communion. The Campbells taught that this was an individual service, and each person should examine himself and not his neighbor. They believed the Lord's Table was set for the Lord's people, and all believers in Christ should have the privilege of remembering Him in His death.

The Baptists required their converts to relate a *"Christian experience"* to the officers of the church or to the congregation, who in return received or rejected them by vote. Mr. Campbell insisted that all who believed that Jesus Christ is the Son of God, and had repented of their sins, should be baptized and become a member of His body.

The Baptists believed that preachers should receive *a direct call from God*, accompanied by a miraculous assurance. The Campbells opposed the miraculous in conversion and also in the call to the ministry. They showed by the example of Timothy that when a young man is consecrated and gifted and of good report among the churches, if he has the desire to preach he should be set apart by the churches to the ministry of the Word.

Through the years these were some of the questions which came to the front. They were discussed in various assemblies. Finally, in

6

1830, the separation became necessary, and from this time forth the group led by the Campbells were known as "Christians," or "Disciples of Christ,' or the "Christian Church," the legal title used being the "Church of Christ."

BARTON W. STONE

CHAPTER XIV

BARTON W. STONE

Every movement develops worthy leaders. Among the most notable of the first half of the nineteenth century was Barton W. Stone, whose work antedates that of the Campbells. He did not meet Alexander Campbell until 1824, and they did not join hands then.

Mr. Stone was born near Port Tobacco, Md., Dec. 24, 1772. His father died when he was a child. When he was seven years of age he accompanied his mother and a large number of brothers and sisters to a new home in Pittsylvania County, Va., in sight of the Blue Ridge Mountains. There he grew to manhood. From his humble forest home he heard the guns of General Greene and Lord Cornwallis in the battle of Guilford Court House, only thirty miles away. He chose law as a profession, and at the age of eighteen entered Guilford Academy, N. C.

DOUBTS ABOUT CALVINISM

As a child, Stone was raised to be a Presbyterian. He had a religious temperament, but the theology of the day seemed so unreasonable and his mind was so befogged that he began to depart from Christian ideas, joining in the youthful pleasures of the world. James McGarey, an evangelist, came to town, held an evangelistic meeting, and led young Stone back to God. For a year he was tossed on the waves of uncertainty, trying to obtain saving faith. He could not understand the strange Calvinistic doctrine of his time. It was so unreasonable and inconsistent. The Westminster Confession of Faith was not consistent with New Testament teaching. Later he said: "Let me here speak when I shall be lying under the clods of the grave: Calvinism is among the heaviest clogs on Christianity in the world. It is a dark mountain between heaven and earth, and is amongst the most discouraging hindrances to sinners from seeking the kingdom of God."

He turned to his Bible, and, studying it carefully, was convinced that God loved the whole world, and the reason that all men are not saved is because of their unbelief; and belief was established in receiving the testimony given in the Word concerning His Son. This is simple New Testament doctrine, and was gladly and freely proclaimed by this young preacher. He now became a candidate for the ministry and accepted the Westminster Confession of Faith only "as far as consistent with the Word of God."

THE CANE RIDGE REVIVAL

He attended a revival in southern Kentucky in 1801, where he studied its work. He saw many people turning to Christ. There were a great many strange things happening that baffle description, and although not in accord with all that was done, he believed it was a good work. That same year his first sermon at Cane Ridge was on the words of the Great Commission, as recorded in Mark 16: 15, 16: "Go ye into all the world, and preach the gospel to every creature. He that believeth and is baptized shall be saved; but he that believeth not shall be damned." And thus another revival began.

This Cane Ridge revival has become notable in history. Twenty-five thousand people camped on the ground until the food supply failed. Three thousand were converted.

BREAK WITH THE PRESBYTERIANS

Mr. Stone was surrounded with strong men—Richard McNemar, John Thompson, John Dunlavy, David Purviance and Robert Marshall. Their preaching was in accordance with the New Testament teaching. It was entirely new to the people. Naturally, it aroused violent opposition, and these preachers were tried for heresy in the synods and presbyteries for preaching un-Calvinistic doctrines. They first tried McNemar, and the other five with him retired to a garden and prayed and consulted and drew up a protest, which was a declaration of independence and a withdrawal from the jurisdiction of the presbytery, but not from the church. When this protest was presented, it enraged that body. In a conference, Matthew Houston, who went to confer with them, saw the righteousness of their position and united with them. These men were suspended because they were accused of having departed from the doctrine and usages of the Presbyterian Church. Stone, however, had been ordained with the understanding that he accepted the confession only "so far as it agreed with the Bible." So they treated him unjustly.

These splendid brethren now organized the Springfield Presbytery. They filed their objections to the Confession of Faith and to all human creeds, and announced their determination to take the Bible alone as their only rule of faith and practice. A year later these men substituted the name "Christian" for "Presbyterian," and published the "Last Will and Testament of the Springfield Presbytery." This was in 1804, at Cane Ridge. Their independent study of the Bible caused them to abandon infant baptism and affusion. The preachers baptized each other, then baptized their congregations. This took place five years before Thomas Campbell issued "The Declaration and Address," and eight years before he and Alexander Campbell were immersed.

FOLLOWERS OF CAMPBELL AND STONE UNITE

CHAPTER XV

FOLLOWERS OF CAMPBELL AND STONE UNITE

When Barton W. Stone and Alexander Campbell met in 1824, they had great esteem for each other, but were far apart in some of their teaching. Mr. Stone could not accept Campbell's teaching on the Holy Spirit, and Campbell questioned the soundness of Stone on the divinity of Christ. What they needed was to get close together, know each other personally and for each to examine the teachings of the other. These things having been done, with a better understanding the differences began to disappear, and they found in the main both stood on the same ground. Near the end of his life Stone said of Campbell: "I will not say there are no faults in Brother Campbell, but there are fewer, perhaps, in him than in any man I know on earth; and over these few my love will throw a veil and hide them forever from view, I am constrained, and willingly constrained, to acknowledge him the greatest promoter of this reformation of any many living."

THE KENTUCKY CONFERENCES

It was the deep desire of both Campbell and Stone that their two groups unite in the common cause. A meeting of representative men from both sides was held at Georgetown, Ky., continuing four days, including Christmas Day of 1831. On New Year's Day another conference was held in Lexington, Ky., in the old meeting house of the "Stone brethren" on Hill Street. Stone and John T. Johnson, Samuel Rogers, G. W. Elley, Jacob Creath and "Raccoon" John Smith were present, with others who were leaders in the movement. This was a mass meeting of all the peoples of both fellowships. They decided to have one man from each to be speaker, setting forth the grounds of union. Barton W. Stone and "Raccoon" John Smith were selected as speakers.

Smith made the first address. He began by saying, "God has bu one people on the earth. He has given to them but one Book, an therein exhorts and commands them to be one family. A union sucl as we plead for, a union of God's people on that one Book, must the be practicable." The only union practicable or desirable must be base on the Word of God as the only rule of faith and practice. He wa careful to differentiate between faith and opinion. He said: "Whil there is but one faith, there may be ten thousand opinions; and henc if Christians are ever to be one, they must be one in faith and no in opinion."

Following the address of Smith, Stone said: "I will not attempt tc introduce any new topic, but will say a few things on the subjects pre sented by my beloved brother." He said: "I have not one objection to the ground laid down by him as the true scriptural basis of union among the people of God, and I am willing to give him now and here my hand." Thus, when these men touched hands, the union of these two great bodies was effected.

All desiring to unite on the principles set forth were requested to signify it by giving each other the hand of fellowship. This having been made known, the audience arose and joined hands. On the next Lord's Day they broke the loaf together at the communion table, for they now had pledged their love and loyalty to a given cause. These two bodies were united in a great plea for Christian union. They exalted the Bible as the only rule of faith and practice. They restored the ordinances of baptism and the Lord's Supper to their rightful place and meaning. They emphasized human responsibility in spiritual things. They made Christ the creed and the foundation of the church, and believed Him to have supreme authority in Christianity.

THE "CHRISTIAN CONNECTION"

Some of the Stone following refused to go with him. They remained, and have through the years had a separate existence. They never became a strong people. In 1932 these people, known as the "Christian Connection," united with the Congregational brotherhood. However, some of their congregations and some individuals refused to go the Congregational way, and united with the Restoration movement.

FOLLOWERS OF CAMPBELL AND STONE UNITE

The Campbell and Stone following would never have united had there not first been an acquaintance. That acquaintance blossomed out into a fine friendship. In all of our debates, discussions, preaching and conferences we need to manifest the spirit that was so clearly shown among this group of leaders who got together in Georgetown and Lexington, Ky., a little more than a hundred years ago. It is a fine art to know how to disagree without being disagreeable.

WALTER SCOTT

CHAPTER XVI

WALTER SCOTT

New occasions not only teach new duties, but they produce great men. The Restoration movement has produced some of the greatest religious leaders in the world. As a people we have not placed a halo around the heads of our great men. We have been too slow to accord them the place they deserve in the galaxy of the great. They had traits of character worthy of emulation.

SCOTCH BACKGROUND

Among these notable leaders no name shines with greater luster than that of Walter Scott. He was born in Moffatt, Dumfrieshire, Scotland, Oct. 31, 1796, one of ten children. He was well-born. His father was a cultured musician, and his mother a beautiful, brilliant woman. The father and mother were both buried in a single grave, the mother dying from shock upon hearing of the death of her husband. Scott was educated in Edinburgh University.

EARLY AMERICAN EXPERIENCES

Scott landed in New York, July 7, 1818, at the age of twenty-two, and took a position as teacher in a classical academy on Long Island. He later came to Pittsburgh, where in 1819 a fellow countryman, George Forrester, gave him a place on the faculty of his school. Forrester's religious life had been influenced by the Haldanes, of Scotland. Forrester and Scott studied the Bible together, with a desire to know the truth. Scott was soon led to give up infant baptism. Later he abandoned sprinkling, and the two men were buried in Christian baptism.

Scott met Alexander Campbell in 1822, at the age of twenty-six years. They had been born and reared in the same religious atmosphere, they were lovers of the Bible, were disgusted with human creeds, and were searching for a bond of union for all Christians. Scott was rather excitable, but had great reason and decided will, and clearly perceived the truth.

CHARACTERISTICS OF HIS PREACHING

It is said that Alexander Campbell never fell below the expectations of his hearers; Scott frequently did, but at times he rose to heights of eloquence which even Mr. Campbell never equaled. There were times when Scott preached with the vigor of Simon Peter on Pentecost. He was an evangelist of power. He was the man needed for those times. Scott preached a Person, and not a system of doctrine, as the object of faith. It was Scott who told the people that the gospel was fourfold:

Facts to be believed.
Commands to be obeyed.
Promises to be enjoyed.
Threatenings to be avoided.

But in its specific application it was fivefold. He used to go about the country visiting the schoolhouses, and would say to the children: "Tell your parents to come to church tonight and hear a man preach on five things." Then, holding up his hand, he would help the children to remember:

Hearing.
Faith.
Repentance.
Confession.
Baptism.

It was Scott who discovered in the Scriptures this fivefold application:

Faith to change the heart.
Repentance to change the life.
Baptism to change the state.
Remission of sins to cleanse from guilt.
The gift of the Holy Spirit to help in the religious life and make one a partaker of the divine nature.

WALTER SCOTT

Scott as an Author

Scott was a forceful writer, and was a favorite contributor to the columns of *The Christian Baptist*, published by Alexander Campbell. He wrote over the signature of "Philip." He preached for the churches in Pittsburgh and Allegheny in 1844, and edited *The Protestant Unionist*. He visited Alexander Campbell in Bethany in the last week of 1855. A little later Scott completed his work, "The Messiahship: or, The Great Demonstration," a book that deserves a place in the libraries of all of our preachers. Alexander Campbell called it "an interesting, edifying, cheering, fascinating volume." Scott died at Mayslick, Ky., Apr. 23, 1861, in his sixty-fifth year.

THE CAMPBELL-WALKER DEBATE

CHAPTER XVII

THE CAMPBELL-WALKER DEBATE

Alexander Campbell proved in five great debates to be the outstanding debater in America. A hundred years ago controversy was unavoidable. Mr. Campbell said more good was accomplished in six days of debate than in a year's preaching. He debated with master minds. Some of these debates have been printed in books, and nothing finer has been produced in defense of the cause he represented, since his day.

His first public debate was with John Walker, a Presbyterian preacher, held at Mt. Pleasant, O., in 1820. Mr. Campbell accepted the challenge to debate. He was not "a rantankerous, argumentative, gadabout," as some have endeavored to depict him. He was a man set for the defense of the faith. On his tombstone at Bethany are these words: "Alexander Campbell, Defender of the Faith." The Campbell-Walker debate was on "Infant Baptism," although attention was given to the entire baptismal question.

CIRCUMCISION AND BAPTISM

Mr. Walker began the debate, favoring infant baptism. His argument was that infant baptism today takes the place of circumcision, and since circumcision was administered to infants, baptism should be administered to them now.

Mr. Campbell argued:

(1) That circumcision was connected with temporal blessings, but baptism was connected with the spiritual.

(2) Circumcision was administered to male children only, but baptism was administered to both sexes.

(3) That circumcision was administered on the eighth day, but baptism was administered at any convenient time.

(4) Circumcision was limited to Abraham's children and those

bought with Abraham's money, but baptism was administered to Gentiles, as well as Jews.

THE HOUSEHOLD BAPTISM

Mr. Walker changed positions and endeavored to prove infant baptism from the household baptisms of the New Testament, arguing that because there was a household there would of necessity be infants therein. There are five cases of household baptism in the Acts of the Apostles, but the study of each of these will show there was not one case where it would be possible for infants to be included, as they could not comply with statements made, which of necessity must refer to believers. Antecedents of baptism are: Hearing, faith, repentance and confession. Infants can qualify in none of these antecedents. Mr. Campbell noted the fact, "*all* the house of Cornelius *feared* God and received the Holy Spirit. Lydia's household was converted as brethren. The word of the Lord was spoken to *all* in the jailer's house, and they *all rejoiced, believing* in God, as well as himself. *All* the household of Crispus believed on the Lord; and the house of Stephanus *addicted themselves to the ministry of the saints.* Now, if these things, which are affirmed of all the baptized, will not apply to infants, then it is plain that no infants were baptized in these homes." Two speeches were given by each man on the action of baptism.

Two years later Mr. Campbell held another debate, with Wm. McCalla, which is also published.

THE CAMPBELL-OWEN DEBATE

CHAPTER XVIII

THE CAMPBELL-OWEN DEBATE

The Campbell-Owen debate took place in Cincinnati, O., Apr. 13-21, 1829.

OWEN AND HIS BELIEFS

Robert Owen was the leading exponent of infidelity in the early part of the nineteenth century. He was the son-in-law of David Dale, an outstanding infidel, who had done much against Christianity in Scotland. The people were reading Robert Owen's "Social System" and were impressed by it. At Kendal, O., and New Harmony, Ind., and other places, communities were turned to atheism, and the religion of Jesus Christ was rejected. They published a paper, advocating their revolutionary views. So popular were Owen's views that the early demise of Christianity was freely predicted.

In *The Christian Baptist* Mr. Campbell published a series of strong articles attacking Robert Owen and the "Social System." Mr. Owen was lecturing in New Orleans, where he challenged the clergy to meet him in discussion, but all were afraid of him. Alexander Campbell learned of the challenge and accepted it. Mr. Owen visited Mr. Campbell in Bethany to talk over the plan of the debate. Walking over the farm, they came to the family burying ground, and Mr. Owen said to Mr. Campbell: "There is one advantage I have over the Christian—I am not afraid to die. Most Christians have fear in death; but if some few items of my business were settled I should be perfectly willing to die at any moment." Mr. Campbell replied: "You say you have no fear in death; have you any hope in death?" Mr. Owen said, "No." "Then," continued Mr. Campbell, pointing to an ox standing near, "you are on a level with that brute. He has fed until he is satisfied and stands in the shade whisking off the flies, and has neither fear nor hope in death." Mr. Owen smiled, but did not attempt to reply.

CONCERNING THE DISCIPLES

The Cincinnati Debate

On Apr. 13, 1829, these two men, distinguished for their positions and ability in debate, met in Cincinnati. On the fifth day Mr. Owen completed the reading of his manuscript. He was unable to follow his opponent in his broad generalizations. He authorized him to proceed without interruption to the close of his argument. Mr. Campbell spoke twelve hours without interruption. Dr. Richardson says, in his biography of Mr. Campbell: "For cogency of argument, comprehensive reach of thought, and eloquence, this address never has been surpassed, if ever equaled. A thoughtful hearer not in sympathy with Mr. Campbell, said at the close, 'I have been listening to a man who seems as one who had been living in all ages'." Mr. Campbell asked all persons in the assembly who believed in the Christian religion to signify by rising, and nearly the entire audience arose. When the other side of the question was put to them, only three persons in the immense audience stood. That debate checked the rising tide of infidelity and greatly strengthened Christianity. The debate added to the prestige of Mr. Campbell. It was published and had a large circulation, and still remains an authority on Christian evidences. Mr. Owen soon abandoned his infidelity schemes in America and returned to the Old World.

Campbell's Popularity Grows

This debate gave to Mr. Campbell the title, "The Defender of the Faith."

After the debate Mr. Owen again accepted of the hospitality of Mr. Campbell, and was treated by him with great kindness, and was urged to abandon infidelity and accept Christ as his Saviour. The appeal moved Mr. Owen to tears, but he did not yield.

The debate brought Mr. Campbell to the forefront of American debaters and gave to him not only the respect and the admiration of multitudes, but made him the religious leader of thousands of people in his day. Later, Mr. Campbell was called to New York City, where on two successive evenings, in their own Tammany Hall, he presented the claims of Christ before multitudes of infidels and drew from them a vote of thanks.

100

THE CAMPBELL-PURCELL DEBATE

9741

CHAPTER XIX

THE CAMPBELL-PURCELL DEBATE

In October, 1836, Alexander Campbell addressed the College of Teachers in Cincinnati, O., on the subject of "Moral Culture." He said that modern civilization, in a large measure, was traceable to the Lutheran Reformation. Bishop Purcell, of the Roman Catholic Church, maintained that "the Reformation had been the cause of all the contention and infidelity in the world." Mr. Campbell challenged him to discuss their differences. The Cincinnati community was eager for the debate, for the Catholics had attempted to exclude the Bible from the public schools.

The debate was agreed upon and began Jan. 13, 1837, continuing seven days. Mr. Campbell affirmed these seven propositions:

1. "The Roman Catholic institution, sometimes called the Holy Apostolic Church, is not, nor was she ever, Catholic, Apostolic or Holy, but is a sect, in the fair import of that word, older than any other sect now existing; not the mother and mistress of all churches, but an apostasy from the only true and Apostolic Church of Christ."

2. "Her notion of Apostolic succession is without any foundation in the Bible, in reason, or in fact; an imposition of the most injurious consequences, built upon unscriptural and antiscriptural traditions, resting wholly upon the opinions of interested and fallible men."

3. "She is not uniform in her faith or united in her members, but unstable and fallible as any other sect or philosophy or religion— Jewish, Turkish or Christian—a confederation of sects under a politico-ecclesiastic head."

4. "She is the Babylon of John, the man of sin of Paul, and the empire of the youngest horn of Daniel's sea monster."

5. "Her notions of purgatory, indulgences, auricular confession, supererogation, etc., essential elements of her system, are immoral in their tendency and injurious to the well-being of society, religious and political."

6. "Notwithstanding her pretensions to have given us the Bible and faith in it, we are perfectly independent of her for our knowledge of that Book and its evidences of divine origin."

7. "The Roman Catholic religion, if infallible and unsusceptible of reformation, as alleged, is essentially anti-American, being opposed to the genius of all free institutions, and positively subversive to them, opposing the general reading of the Scriptures and the diffusion of useful knowledge among the whole community, so essential to liberty and the permanency of good government."

Outcome of the Debate

Bishop Purcell was an opponent worthy of Mr. Campbell. But the latter was well prepared for the debate. He had lived in priest-ridden Ireland, where he was familiar with Catholic customs. He was a thorough student of the history of the church, and therefore stood on familiar ground in this debate. He said in an opening sentence, "I come not to advocate the particular tenets of any sect, but to defend the great cardinal principles of Protestantism." The Protestant clergy of Cincinnati and vicinity were most hearty in their commendation of Mr. Campbell's addresses. Among the number was Lyman Beecher, father of Henry Ward Beecher. This debate did much to dispel the prejudices and criticism against the plea for the restoration of the church of the New Testament. At a mass meeting, following the debate, resolutions were adopted, declaring that "It is the unanimous opinion of this meeting that the cause of Protestantism has been fully sustained throughout the discussion."

The debate was published and had a large sale, and remains to this day one of the strongest defenses of Protestant Christianity that has been set forth.

Campbell's Last Debate

Mr. Campbell's last debate was with N. L. Rice, a Presbyterian, in Lexington, Ky., beginning Nov. 15, 1843, and continuing sixteen days. This debate was on the subject of "Christian Baptism." The debate was printed in a volume of more than nine hundred pages and had a large sale. It still remains a classic on the subject.

EDUCATION

CHAPTER XX

EDUCATION

Jesus called twelve men, who walked with Him during His ministry. These were students in His school, preparing to preach His Word after He ascended to the Father. The Christian religion is a teaching religion, making its appeal to the head and to the heart. In Romans, tenth chapter, Paul said: "Whosoever shall call upon the name of the Lord shall be saved. How then shall they call on Him in whom they have not believed? And how shall they believe in Him whom they have not heard? And how shall they hear without a preacher? And how shall they preach except they be sent?" And one may well add to these questions of Paul, How shall they preach without preparation?

Alexander Campbell was a student, a preacher, and an educator. Knowing full well the days of inspiration ceased with the apostles, he saw the necessity of a trained ministry if the gospel is to be preached intelligently to all the world.

In 1818 Mr. Campbell established in his home, "Buffalo Seminary," the purpose of which was to help the local community and train young men for the ministry. The school was discontinued after a few years. The demands upon his time, with the lack of interest on the part of young men to make preparation, served as reasons for closing the school.

THE FIRST COLLEGES

In 1840 the charter for Bethany College was obtained. The first gift was a thousand dollars, from W. B. Pendleton, of Virginia. A large brick building was erected. On September 18 Mr. Campbell was elected president, and May 10 of the next year four teachers were added to the faculty. They were: W. K. Pendleton, Andrew F. Ross, Charles Stewart and Robert Richardson. October 21 the school opened and has maintained yearly schedules until this day.

Bethany College was the first college to introduce the Bible as the chief textbook. Alexander Campbell said: "The formation of moral character and the culture of the heart is the supreme end of education; an immoral man is uneducated. The blasphemer, the profane swearer, the liar, and the calumniator are uneducated persons." He gave a Bible lecture each morning in the college, which gave the students a clear and comprehensive conception "of the doings of God in the creation and government of the world." Every great school must have a great personality, and Bethany had hers in Alexander Campbell. The roll call of Bethany will bring response from men who have been leaders in various walks of life in our nation—educators, preachers, authors and teachers. Here are a few: Thomas Munnell, O. A. Burgess, Robert Graham, Moses E. Lard, Alexander Proctor, F. D. Power, John W. McGarvey, Charles L. Loos, W. H. Woolery, A. McLean, E. V. Zollars, Russell Errett, and hundreds of others whose lives and work have been a blessing to humanity.

In 1836 Bacon College was founded, at Georgetown, Ky., with Walter Scott as president pro tem. The launching of this enterprise was due to the initiative of John T. Johnson. In 1840, the year the charter was taken out for Bethany, it was moved to Harrodsburg, and James Shannon became president. Later the school was moved to Lexington and took the name of Kentucky University, but is now known as Transylvania College, and is the oldest college west of the Alleghenies. Through a merger with another institution its history dates back to 1798, with George Washington, John Adams, Aaron Burr and General Lafayette contributing to the first endowment fund. Henry Clay was at one time a member of the faculty, and Jefferson Davis was for four years a student. The Bible College connected with Transylvania has prepared many of our men for the ministry. It has had great educators in the persons of Robert Milligan, J. W. McGarvey, I. B. Grubbs, C. L. Loos. It is claimed that nearly six thousand of our preachers around the world have received all or a part of their education at Lexington.

LATER EDUCATIONAL INSTITUTIONS

In 1849 the Western Reserve Eclectic Institute was organized at Hiram, O. James A. Garfield (the twentieth President of the United

States) was the second president of the school. In 1867 the Institute became Hiram College.

Butler College, Indianapolis, Ind., was chartered in 1850. It was first known as Northwestern Christian University.

In 1855 Eureka College, Eureka, Ill., was launched, under the title of Walnut Grove Academy, now know as Eureka. Later Abbington College, of Illinois, became a part of Eureka College.

In 1853 Christian University was organized at Canton, Mo. This is said to be the first school in the United States to grant equal privileges to men and women. It occupies an eminence overlooking the Mississippi River.

About the same time Oskaloosa College, at Oskaloosa, Ia., was founded, and later merged with Drake University, Des Moines, one of the largest schools of our people at the present time.

Texas Christian University is located at Ft. Worth, Tex. It is the outgrowth of Add-Ran College.

Johnson Bible College, the school of evangelists, is located at Kimberlin Heights, Tenn.; founded by Ashley Johnson in 1893.

Oklahoma Christian University, now known as Phillips University, is located at Enid, Okla. This school was established by E. V. Zollars, for many years the president of Hiram College, and one of the greatest college presidents our brotherhood ever produced. T. W. Phillips, of New Castle, Pa., was the generous donor who assured the perpetuation of this school.

Virginia Christian College is located at Lynchburg, Va., and was founded by Josephus Hopwood in 1903.

Many other schools are conducted under our auspices. Some are: Atlantic Christian College, Wilson, N. C.; Northwest Christian College, Eugene, Ore.; Louisville Christian Bible School, Louisville, Ky.; Milligan College, Milligan, Tenn.; Minnesota Bible University, Minneapolis, Minn.; Chapman College, Los Angeles, Calif.; Cincinnati Bible Seminary, Cincinnati, O.; Christian Normal Institute, Grayson, Ky.; Cotner College, Lincoln, Neb.

Three other schools, while in a measure not identified with any religious body, are deserving mention. They were launched and directed by presidents who were members of the Christian Church, and who trained many men for the ministry. We refer to Ohio Northern University, Ada, O., H. S. Lehr, president and founder,

109

now a Methodist institution; Tri-State College, Angola, Ind., L. M. Sniff, president; Valparaiso University, Valparaiso, Ind., H. M. Brown, president. All three presidents are dead.

There are more than fifty able preachers proclaiming the Word with power who received their training in Phillips Bible Institute at Canton, O., a school that was called into existence in 1914, and was removed to Valparaiso, Ind., in 1918, and there had a speedy death.

A few Bible chairs have been established in connection with the state universities. The purpose was good, but the results have not in all respects reached to the expectations of the promoters.

LIBERTY

CHAPTER XXI

LIBERTY

When the movement began one hundred twenty-five years ago to unite Christian people by the restoration of the church of the New Testament, the church had passed through the long years of the apostasy and many years of denominational and sectarian narrowness. The body of believers in Christ was cut up into segments. The bigotry of the age was most repellant. To break the shackles that held Christian people in bondage and to move out with the privilege of exercising their own minds in relation to the great truths of the Bible, were the realization of a vision splendid.

Liberty, Not License

Our people realized then, and still proclaim a liberty that is consistent with the teaching of the Scriptures. They repudiate overlords and are content to be panoplied with the simplicity of the Scriptures themselves. They recognize the authority of Jesus Christ and that delegated authority of Christ to the apostles. This authority is expressed in Holy Writ. They believe the words of the inspired writers to be as authoritative as the words of Christ Himself, for, "Holy men of God spake as they were moved by the Holy Spirit." The utterances of the inspired writers and those of the Christ are in full accord; therefore, the Scriptures are our rule of faith and practice. That is why they take the position that "where the Bible speaks, we speak; and where the Bible is silent, we are silent."

Certain things are fundamental, and while we are not, strictly speaking, "Fundamentalists," as the term is frequently used, we do believe in the fundamental or essential principles of the gospel. In all things actually essential to the organization, maintenance, and well-being of the church, we plead for unity. In all things not essential we grant to others and ask for ourselves the widest liberty.

113

CONCERNING THE DISCIPLES

We believe in tolerance equal to that of the Christ and the apostles. We fully recognize there is an intolerance which must also be maintained. We would be as intolerant as the Christ and as tolerant as He. It would be unscriptural to tolerate doctrines not of the Scripture's advocacy, therefore we must hold to the Scriptures as our guide.

The great questions, such as the fact of God, the Deity of Jesus Christ, the Lordship of Jesus, the inspiration of the Bible, and the Bible as one's rule of faith and practice, the answer to the question, "What must I do to be saved?", the great plan of human redemption, the ordinances—baptism and the Lord's Supper—the name to be worn, the creed to be believed, the purpose of the church and its organization, clearly have been set forth in the Scriptures, and to the Scriptures we return for the solution of these problems. If we are in accord with scriptural teaching, what more can be desired? To add to the Scriptures is presenting too much. To subtract from them we present too little. To accept them as they are is sufficient. That is why the Scriptures alone are accepted as the discipline for the church. No creed but Christ, no discipline but the Word of God will eliminate many differences and serve as a bond of union among believers.

CONGREGATIONAL FREEDOM

This freedom enjoyed by our people is a priceless boon, a heritage not to be despised. It looms large in the words of Jesus, who said, "Ye shall know the truth and the truth shall make you free." We are not dominated by synods, presbyteries, councils, popes, conventions, missionary societies, or publishing houses. The church in a given community stands as a free and independent organization, fashioned after the church of the New Testament order. All the churches should co-operate in great works, as the members of a local congregation should co-operate in the work of the church. Missionary societies are agencies, not overlords, through which the church may work for the evangelization of the world and the furtherance of altruistic interests. Publishing houses are servants of the church, depending upon the church for support. Conventions are great inspi-

ational gatherings, where brethren meet on common ground to discuss the things of the kingdom, to plan, to pray, to join hands
and heart in a great cause. There should be co-operation with every
good work.

The disciples of the early day were marked by their fellowship,
co-operative spirit, and great interest in a common cause. When that
spirit returns among our people and the fear of ecclesiastical organization is put to rout, and we stand united on the Scriptures and the
Scriptures only in the great cause of human redemption and the
edification of the saints, we shall do well.

CHRISTIAN UNION

CHAPTER XXII

CHRISTIAN UNION

From the first, churches of Christ have desired Christian union. It took some time in the beginning of the last century for the leaders in the Restoration movement to find solid ground on which to stand on the union question. Co-operation, federation, and amalgamation were insufficient. Any suggested man-made basis was found to be inadequate.

With far-seeing eye, the leaders came to see the only basis for union is that of the Scriptures. They went back to the church of the New Testament—the church that was established and directed through the agency of the Holy Spirit. They perceived if we can reproduce this church in all its essential qualities we can give to the world the basis for Christian unity. They drew a sharp distinction between essentials and nonessentials.

Agreement can not be reached on matters of opinion. Where the Scriptures speak, we give heed and follow.

THE DOCTRINE

From this reasoning it is clearly seen that the first necessity is to decide upon the essential features upon which Christian people can agree before there can be Christian unity. The first thing required is that one shall be in Christ. If all are in Christ they are united, but if one be in Christ, and another out of Christ, there is no unity, hence the first requirement is to ascertain what is demanded of an individual to put him into Christ; or, in other words, to make him a Christian after the New Testament pattern. New Testament evangelism clearly sets forth these steps: hearing the Word, believing in the Christ, repenting of one's sins, confessing the Christ, and being baptized into the Christ. This is not man-made; it is the plan set forth by the Holy Spirit and can not be denied.

CONCERNING THE DISCIPLES

THE ORDINANCES

There are two ordinances—Christian baptism, and the Lord's Supper. Christian baptism is clearly shown in the Scriptures to be the burial of a penitent believer in water in the name of Jesus Christ, for remission of sins.

The Lord's Supper was ordained by the Christ for His followers, to be kept in memory of Him, and "the disciples came together upon the first day of the week to break bread." In restoring the church of the New Testament this ordinance must be restored, both in form and spirit.

THE NAME

In union there must be an agreement as to the name. Only a scriptural name can be accepted, therefore we search the Scriptures to ascertain the name by which the institution known as the church and its membership were known. In union all must accept the same creed. We therefore present the creed that needs no revision, the creed which all do accept, the all-comprehensive creed, the living Creed, which is the Christ, the Son of the living God.

THE DISCIPLINE

In Christian union all must be disciplined by the same discipline. Paul tells us, "All Scripture given by the inspiration of God is profitable for doctrine, for reproof, for correction, for instruction in righteousness, that the man of God may be perfect and thoroughly furnished unto all good works." To have more than the Scriptures offer is having too much—to have less is not having enough; to have exactly what the Scriptures offer meets the requirements. So the Scriptures themselves become our rule of faith and action.

THE POLITY

The polity of the church is clearly set forth in the New Testament Scriptures. It can not be improved upon. If that organization was given by men led by the Holy Spirit it would seem that that organization would be sufficient for the church in the world today, for the mind of man will make no improvement over that set forth by inspired men who spake as the Holy Spirit gave them utterance.

There is nothing narrow about this position. We are asking no one to accept the mandates of men. We are presenting no human requirements for keeping the "unity of the Spirit in the bonds of peace." Laying aside all teaching that is foreign to the Scriptures, departing from the doctrines of men and the counsel of assemblies, the men of the early part of the last century and those who follow them, simply present "the one Lord, the one faith, the one baptism," and invite all believers in Christ to step out of their narrow circles onto the broad platform presented by the Christ and inspired men.

CHAPTER XXIII

THE PROFITABLENESS OF CHRISTIAN UNION

Christian union was a fact, not a theory, in the first century. Why should it not be a fact today? Christian union is sensible. Division is unscriptural and antiscriptural, harmful, weakens the church, and is unreasonable. The Scriptures furnish the basis for unity.

To restore the church as it was in the first century, in all essentials, and thus have unity, will be most profitable to the edvancement of the kingdom of God.

Nothing can hope to prosper greatly and permanently that is contradictory to the will of God, as expressed in the simple teaching of the Scriptures.

PROMOTES COMMUNITY UNITY

A united church will solve the overchurched problem. Villages and many rural districts, as well as cities, are overchurched. Frequently a village with a population ranging from six to twelve hundred people will have three or four churches. The forces are divided and money is wasted in fostering separate organizations. There are many duplications of effort, all of which can be avoided by having in that community one church. The one church will create and maintain good will among the membership and make a strong appeal to the community. United forces will be set toward a common goal. Duplication of effort will be avoided, useless machinery, with corresponding overhead, can be eliminated, and instead of working to keep alive a denominational body, all will work to save souls and to edify the saints.

The ill will engendered in overchurched communities is a distinctive setback to Christianity in that community. Jesus Christ taught love, not hate. Too much of the rivalry that exists among churches is caused by denominational pride and interest, rather than the wider interests in the kingdom of God.

Many a church is dying with the dry rot of respectability, and preachers are merely existing on the feeble support accorded by the church. One church in a given community, where all the forces are united, can employ a good preacher, be served by a strong choir, organize in a businesslike manner, and backed by the spirit of God, can go forth in the conquest over sin and win the community to Christ.

The divided church results in divided homes, which precipitates dying interest in religious activity. What a spectacle is presented when the father goes to one church, the mother to another, and frequently the children to another. They forget Paul's statement to the church at Corinth, "Let there be no divisions among you, but all speak the same thing." Divisions not infrequently cause a family to lose all interest in godly things. Divisions cause bitter strife in the community and nullify the effects of gospel preaching.

PROMOTES MISSIONARY IMPETUS

The church is playing at the game of world-wide missions. It has but touched the fringe of the garment of Christian benevolence, and at the same time is wasting millions of dollars per year on keeping up needless churches, all of which is in direct opposition to the teaching of the Bible. Christ prayed for unity that the world might believe that God had sent Him. A united church can evangelize the world. A divided church can never do it completely and successfully.

PROMOTES SOCIAL PROGRESS

A united church can affect the economic, political, moral and spiritual conditions of the world, for, "in union there is strength." With present conditions, it is difficult to get a united voice from the followers of Christ on the great problems of the day. Too much jealousy exists among the various bodies of believers. Politicians will give ear to the great voice of the church when it speaks unitedly. The forces that wink at every attempt to usher in a better moral situation will tremble when the church speaks and acts as one body.

THE PROFITABLENESS OF CHRISTIAN UNION

Promotes the Cause of Christ

During the World War the church received no credit for anything it did in that titanic struggle. The credit went to the Y. M. C. A. and K. of C. and the Salvation Army, because the church was divided, and the divided church was compelled to make itself effective through these forces, which were entirely dependent upon the brains, the brawn and the gifts and consecration of the various bodies of Christendom. A united church would have asserted itself and made known to the world its power. Instead, even to this day people refer to what the Y. M. C. A., the K. of C. and the Salvation Army did, and then remark, "They were more influential than the church in the days of the war, and my support goes to those institutions." The facts are, those institutions would have been powerless had the church not furnished the funds and the workers through their channels.

Promotes Virile Preaching

A united church will stress the proper note. Much of the preaching today is on disputed subjects, and needless controversy is introduced into religious worship. To preach the gospel and to defend the "faith once for all delivered unto the saints" are quite different from defending unscriptural and antiscriptural positions. The great doctrines of the Bible ought to be stressed continually. They make for faith, stimulate activity in Christian work and develop Christian graces.

Christian union is in the air and is the desire of multitudes in the various denominational folds today.

HINDRANCES TO UNITY

CHAPTER XXIV

HINDRANCES TO UNITY

In previous chapters we have stated the New Testament basis for Christian union, and have shown the profitableness of such union. We now consider hindrances to unity.

IGNORANCE OF THE SCRIPTURES

Ignorance of the Scriptures is a hindrance. Many people study the Bible with a bias. They are prejudiced and read to substantiate their position, rather than to find the truth. The masses of the people are unacquainted with church history. They do not know the various ramifications and the treacherous, tangled roads along which the church has come through nineteen hundred years. Many are not aware that there was but one church at the beginning. They have never attempted to measure the church to which they belong with the measuring rod of the New Testament church. They are depending upon the word from the pulpit in all matters of religion, and the pulpit has not always sounded a clear note. A careful reading of the Scriptures should be sufficient to convince the thoughtful reader that divisions are condemned by the inspired men who wrote the Scriptures, and common sense should show them through their observations round about that the divided church can not save the world.

IGNORANCE OF CHURCH HISTORY

Ignorance possessed by one denomination concerning all the others is a hindrance to unity. If all Protestantism would get together and frankly, fairly and fearlessly, but kindly, consider their points of agreement they will be surprised to see how much uniformity obtains in matters of faith and practice. Many of the differences are inconsequential. In the main, they agree on a thousand things, where

131

they disagree on one, and very frequently that is not an essential.
Divisions, in some cases, began with the thought of stressing some
great truth. The body advocating that truth soon developed into a
denomination. By and by other bodies accepted the same truth
to the end that in the main, many of the conditions that brought
about divisions in the church have disappeared, but the separate bodies
keep on, with no reason for their separate existence.

High Regard for Competition

Competition among the churches is sometimes offered as a legiti-
mate reason for division. The remark is made, "Competition is the life
of business." And it might also be said, "Competition sometimes
kills business." Nowhere is this seen more clearly than among the
churches. If the church desires competition to motivate it and keep
it busy, it has plenty of it in fighting the world, the flesh, and the
devil. The difficulty is competition means one church being arrayed
against another. The church has all it can possibly do to fight rampant sins, without turning the guns on another body of believers. This
competition has split churches, disrupted families, created havoc in
the community, made bitter enemies of one-time friends, and closed
many a church door. The devil likes that sort of thing.

Denominational Leaders

Denominational leaders are frequently to blame for division. The
great body of church people are sick of division. They would like
to come together, all assembling in the one fold, under the leader-
ship of the one Shepherd, but leaders sometimes interfere. They
talk much about unity, but are not at home when you get down
to the real business of unity on the New Testament basis. There is
a certain pride in their denomination, which is taken by many leaders.
Traditions hang about their church as leaves cover the tree in the
springtime. The prejudice which has been inherited is no small factor
in fostering division. There is a certain amount of prejudice to be
found harbored in the heart of one religious body against another.
And until people are taught the truth and see the truth these barriers
will not be burned away easily.

HINDRANCES TO UNITY

CORPORATE AND MONEYED INTERESTS

Moneyed interests are opposed to the merging of the denominations into the one body—the church of the living God. Each denomination has spent great sums of money in publishing houses, missionary agencies, hospitals, asylums and educational institutions. In any case of unity there has to be an adjustment, and a good many leaders are unwilling to step aside that the proper adjustments may be made. Such selfishness is a deterrent factor in the cause of unity.

THE ALIBI OF "TEMPERAMENT"

It is argued that people need various denominations because of the different temperaments, but the strange thing about that argument is that in no one denomination do you find just one temperament, but every denomination has all temperaments under the sun in it; so denominationalism is not necessary to furnish a pigeon-hole for separate temperaments. The unity desired will be on the essential things. When it comes to the manner of worship, music, style of architecture, and all of those nonessential items where opinion can predominate, the people rule and will arrange their program according to their desire. It is simply on the fundamental things—the essentials—where the Lord has spoken, that we must not permit opinions.

It will be a perfect day when all believers in Christ—Greek and Roman Catholic and Protestant can unite. But it is useless to think of that day until Protestantism unites its divided forces into the one great body described, in doctrine and polity, in the New Testament. A united Protestantism will have greater force in attempting to bring the Jew to Christ, and it certainly is folly for a divided Protestant church to make overtures to Anglican and Catholic for unity.

Peter Ainslie, in *The Christian Quarterly* of October, 1913, says: "The greatest hindrance to union today is ungodliness in the church, in the form of bigotry, sectarianism, pride, meanness, history and self-righteousness. Upon these issues divisions have come, and until they are scourged out of the portals of the church, union is impossible. There is not a communion in Christendom that is not infected with this disease, some in one form, and some in another, but in all there is an element of ungodliness that will poison the church if not cured."

133

CHAPTER XXV

THE PRESENT STATUS OF CHRISTIAN UNION

All religious bodies are in agreement that unity is desirable. All would vote for unity tomorrow if they could effect it by voting to give up nothing. Any one camp would be willing to receive the other camps into its own if all the others would just get up and move in unconditionally. The problem is, How can unity be effected?

THE RESTORATION MOVEMENT

There are leaders among all the divisions who are outstanding exponents and are eloquent advocates of unity, but there are few who are willing to go back to the beginning and restore the church as it was in the first century. This movement to bring about unity on the New Testament basis was launched Sept. 7, 1809, when Thomas Campbell wrote "The Declaration and Address." Through the years the Restoration movement has presented this New Testament basis to the religious world. The trouble is, we have not covered enough territory, have not reached enough people, and with all of our preaching the religious world is largely unacquainted with our plea.

THE SO-CALLED "CATHOLIC" MOVEMENTS

The religious journals, many of the pulpits, and all federated movements discuss freely and frequently the desirability and the necessity of unity. The Roman Catholic Church, the Greek Catholic, and the Anglican have written volumes upon the subject. The Catholic Church would be glad to have unity if all would become Catholics. The Episcopalian makes a plea for unity by all becoming Episcopalians.

The big work ahead of us just now is to unite Protestant Christianity, for Catholic, Anglican and Protestant can not unite until

10

Protestantism first presents a solid front. It is therefore with the unity of Protestantism we are most concerned.

FEDERATION

One of the plans suggested is that of federation. It is a compromise by which denominations are attempting to work together without disturbing the denominational status. It merely furnishes a working basis, but is not unity in the New Testament sense. In 1905 a general conference was called in Carnegie Hall, New York City, in which the majority of Protestant bodies in the United States had representation. Out of this conference was born "The Federal Council of the Churches of Christ in America." Federation is purely sectarian. It recognizes divisions and fosters them. It merely presents a plan for friendly relationship among the denominations.

THE COMMUNITY CHURCH

The "community church" has been presented as a solution. The "community church' is exactly what we desire, provided that church is built entirely on the New Testament basis, but the so-called "Community Church" consists simply of a group of folk coming from different denominations who agree to live together and work together. In reality, it adds one more to the body of denominations. It grants the privilege to each communicant to believe what he pleases and to do as he pleases. It is quite a long distance from the pattern of the New Testament Church.

THE LAMBETH QUADRILATERAL

In 1853 the bishops of the Protestant Episcopal Church appointed a commission to confer with the Protestant churches in America concerning Christian union. In 1880 the bishops of the same church published what they called "The Solidarity of the Catholic Episcopate." In 1886 they presented a four-sided proposition of union, known as the quadrangular basis, which was endorsed by the Lambeth Conference in London in 1888. This is known as "The Lambeth Quadrilateral." It accepted the Old and New Testaments as the rule and ultimate standard of faith. The Apostles' Creed was presented as the baptismal symbol, and the Nicene Creed as the sufficient statement of the Christian church. They accepted baptism and the Lord's Supper as the two "sacraments" ordained by Christ. They took a stand for the historic episcopate to be adapted locally to the church. In other words, it was an invitation from the Episcopal Church to all denominations to become members of that church. That, of course, can never be, for the Episcopal Church stands too far removed from the pattern in the New Testament.

UNION OF CHURCH FAMILIES

One of the hopeful signs today is that the walls are crumbling between the divisions of a given denomination. There are twelve kinds of Presbyterians, seventeen kinds of Methodists, twenty-two kinds of Lutherans, and several kinds of Baptists, as well as many divisions among other denominations. The fact that in many of these there is a gesture towards breaking the divided walls augurs well for a better day.

FACTORS WHICH MAKE FOR UNITY

There are factors which make for union today. The failure of the divided church to accomplish the greatest good is opening the eyes of Christian people. The more one studies the Scripture the more he is convinced that a united church will be the answer to the prayer of our Lord, as recorded in the seventeenth chapter of John. The financial situation will help to drive congregations together, especially in the overchurched communities. The Christian Endeavor, W. C. T. U., Y. M. C. A., Y. W. C. A., and other Christian organizations are bringing people into closer relationship and thereby helping them to understand one another better. This is creating a desire for closer fellowship, which is a step toward the desired unity. The condition on the foreign field calls for unity. The non-Christian world cares nothing about the ecclesiastical differences of Christian nations. Interdenominational controversies will not win the heathen to Jesus Christ. The Westminster Confession, the Augsburg Confession, and all the other confessions are entirely foreign to the presentation of the simple gospel.

139

CONCERNING THE DISCIPLES

More than a third of a century ago Dr. Anson G. Chester, an aged minister of the Presbyterian Church, heard Z. T. Sweeney in an evangelistic meeting in Buffalo, N. Y. At the age of seventy-five years this preacher identified himself with the church of Christ. To him the preaching had been new. The position, likewise, was new, and the whole plan was revealed to him as the will of God. Having heard the message for two weeks, the night he was received into the church he said: "You people have the greatest thing in the world, and you are the stingiest with it." As a people we have a great mission; that is, to proclaim this New Testament basis of Christian unity to all the world. This must be done in preaching, on the printed page, and in conference.

HAVE WE OUTGROWN "THE PLEA"?

CHAPTER XXVI

HAVE WE OUTGROWN "THE PLEA"?

To some "the plea" seems to be an antiquated term. Until recent years it was upon the lips of all the preachers and teachers in the brotherhood. One hundred twenty-five years ago it was presented without fear or favor.

What Is "the Plea"?

What is "the plea"? It is stated in the seventeenth chapter of John's Gospel by Christ, when He prayed "that they all may be one." This is the unanswered prayer of Jesus. He made no plans for divisions. Sectarianism was foreign to His plans and purpose. The disciples were commanded by Paul to "keep the unity of the spirit in the bonds of peace." After the apostasy—the falling away of the church— the long thousand years of the Dark Ages and the Reformation, men were called back to the pure Word of God, with the hope that in the restoration of the church of the New Testament in doctrine, polity and life, the union of that church in the first century would be restored. So, "the plea" is for the unity of all believers in Christ, and the plan is the restoration of the church of Christ as described in the New Testament.

Its Aim Not Accomplished

Now, the question—have we outgrown "the plea"? If we have outgrown it, it must follow the believers are already united, or there has been a change in the revealed will of God. A glimpse of the religious world refutes the statement we have unity, and there is no place where the will of God has been expressed as being out of sympathy with the earnest, challenging prayer of the only begotten Son of God.

143

CONCERNING THE DISCIPLES

MANY HAVE NOT HEARD IT

The need of unity is apparent, and the way to unity is accessible and adequate. Some have said: "We have outgrown 'the plea' because it has not up to date succeeded in uniting all the divided forces of Christendom." Be it remembered that the divided forces have not all heard "the plea." Too many of our own people do not know it, and many of our preachers seldom, if ever, preach it. One might as well argue as to the failure of the gospel to save people because all in the world have not been saved. All have not heard the gospel, and many have received a mutilated gospel—besides, there is the world, the flesh, and the devil against which the gospel must contend. The efficacy of the gospel must not be questioned because all who have heard it have not accepted it. We have not outgrown the gospel and never will outgrow it, and so long as "the plea" for the unity of all believers in Christ is a part of the gospel we have not outgrown that.

IT IS AS ENDURING AS THE WORD

The opinions of men will cease to be. One generation outgrows the customs of the preceding generation. The years add knowledge unto knowledge. Man becomes wiser with the passing days. We have outgrown the ox cart, the stage coach, the horse and carriage. This is an automobile age, a period of rapid transit. These methods of travel are the product of man's thinking and ingenuity. Many of the old doctrines formerly proclaimed have been outgrown, because those doctrines were the speculations and opinions of men. The student has become wiser in his interpretation and understanding of Scriptures. But we have not outgrown the "thus saith the Lord" of the Bible. Regardless of man's thinking on any given Scripture, the great facts of the Scriptures stand unchanged. Man, in his thinking, not the Word of God, changes. "Heaven and earth shall pass away, but my word shall not pass away," saith Jehovah.

IT IS AS ENDURING AS THE CHURCH

"The plea" is ineffective without the plan, and the plan is to restore the original organic church of the New Testament. In that

144

restoration several things must be considered—first, the Christ must be restored to His place of authority and divine Lordship. We have not outgrown the Christ, although some would strip Him of His deity and make Him the son of Joseph, and not the Son of God; but the fact of Christ remains, the Scriptures entirely substantiate all His claims. We can not outgrow that great item of our faith.

The Word of God is our rule of faith and practice. Some may have become so wise in their own conceit as not to need the Scriptures any longer. Such a one will also cease to lead the people to the Christ. We are commanded to "preach the gospel." We have nothing to preach but the gospel. We have not outgrown that gospel, which is "the power of God unto salvation to every one that believeth."

We have not outgrown the New Testament laws of spiritual birth. Babes born into this world today come through the observance of the natural laws of generation and birth. There has been no change in those laws from the days of Adam until now. We have not outgrown those natural laws. He who gave the natural law is also author of the spiritual, and the spiritual law of birth is declared by Jesus when speaking to Nicodemus in the third chapter of John. He said: "Verily, verily, I say unto thee, except one be born of water and the Spirit he cannot enter into the kingdom of God." We can not outgrow it. And it has its place in "the plea" we present.

Have we outgrown the ordinances—baptism and the Lord's Supper? They are ordained of Christ, to whom all authority hath been given. He has never bestowed upon any man the right to make null and void those ordinances. Baptism is a part of the new birth, and so long as that birth is spiritually lawful just that long baptism has its place in the divine plan of appropriating Christ's death unto the salvation of men. The Lord's Supper is a beautiful memorial by which we remember Christ's death, and it is to be in force until He comes. His second coming remains in the future, hence we have not outgrown that ordinance.

"The plea" presents the Christ as the creed that needs no revision. So long as the church stands, the creed, its foundation, its principle, must abide. He is the universal creed, profound enough for the wisest, simple enough for the unlearned. Upon Him there must be universal agreement. If the creed were to be outgrown what could be accepted in His stead? The Christ has no superiors, and He has no peers. His name is above every name. We certainly have not outgrown the Creed of Christendom.

Our Obligation to Present It

If we have not outgrown "the plea" with all of its attending elements, what shall we do with it? There is just one obligation, and that is to present it. If properly presented it will be kindly received. It must be intelligently understood by every preacher of the great brotherhood and by the men and women of the local churches. The good news should be broadcast to the ends of the earth. This "plea" is the unanswered prayer of our Lord. When that prayer is answered peace among the people of God will flow like a gentle river. Then, truly, will "the desert blossom as the rose" and "the trees will clap their hands for joy."

"The plea" has made the brotherhood. Its proclamation is the only reason we have for existence. To cease proclaiming it opens the gate for a brotherhood to disappear. With the crying need of the hour, when faithful believers in Christ are seeking the light of liberty and are trying to throw off the yoke of narrow sectarianism, we should take no position on the misty mountain tops, wrapped in the mantle of isolation, but stand before the people, and with trumpet voice present "the plea" as the solution of the perplexing problem of division, and as a healing ointment for the hurt of a divided church.

THE DIVINITY OF CHRIST

CHAPTER XXVII

THE DIVINITY OF CHRIST

The Restoration movement has placed needed emphasis upon several cardinal doctrines of the New Testament. A consideration of these doctrines will not be amiss in this book. Among these the divinity and Lordship of Christ is the chiefest.

There have been six views through the ages, held by men, concerning the Christ. He has been classified as (1) a myth, (2) a fictious character, (3) an impostor, (4) a fanatic, (5) a good man, and (6) the divine Son of God. We shall not consider the first four in this chapter—they are too silly to consider. It has been demonstrated many times that He is not a myth, nor a fictitious character. The study of His life, as recorded by Matthew, Mark, Luke and John proves He was neither an impostor nor a fanatic. Thinkers today put Him in one of two categories—He is either the son of Joseph or the Son of God.

The Fact of Christ

The fact that Jesus lived, and that He lived in the time in which the Gospel writers declare He lived, needs no proof. Men still visit the land of His birth, where He lived, labored and loved. The Lord's Day, the Lord's Supper and Christian baptism owe their origin to Him. His birth changed the calendar, and every letter we address is addressed in the "year of our Lord." The question with which we are concerned is this, Was He the son of Joseph, or the Son of God?

The Claims of Christ

If He is the son of Joseph, then He is a mere man, not Deity. In this case He is inexplainable, for He can be accounted for only on the basis of His deity. If a mere man, why has there not been produced through all the years another man His superior or His

149

equal? He stands forth as the lonely Man in His isolation, fo no other has ever approached Him. If He was merely a man, the He was not a good man, for He made certain claims which, if un true, brand Him as one deceived or a deceiver. Note these claims He said, "I am the way, the truth, and the life." Again, "N man cometh unto the Father but by me." "I and the Father ar one." He declared Himself to be "the only begotten Son of God." He said He performed miracles by the power of God. He declared He would be the Judge of all the earth, and that in the judgmen the people of the world would stand before Him. He said, "Befor Abraham was, I am." He declared, "He that hath seen me hath seen the Father"; and, "I am in the Father and the Father in me." These claims were either false or true. If false, He was not a good man. If true, He is more than a mere man, and must be divine.

THE PERFECTION OF CHRIST

If Jesus were a mere man, who can account for His knowledge His ability and His perfect life? The people who knew Him and had seen Him grow from childhood to manhood, were astonished at His doctrine and marveled at the knowledge of one who had not been educated in their schools, and exclaimed, "Whence hath this man knowledge?" Those who were sent to arrest Him declared, "Never a man spake like this man." He said, "Which of you convicteth me of sin?" And Pilate said, "I find no fault in him." He was the one man of all the world who stood forth without sin.

There is an abundance of proof that Jesus Christ is what He claimed to be—*the* Son of God. He was not *a* son, but was *the* Son of God. He is the only begotten Son. All other believers in Christ are adopted sons, hence Paul said: "We have the spirit of adoption, whereby we cry, Abba-Father." John tells us: "He came to his own and his own received him not. But as many as received him, to them gave he power to become the sons of God."

THE MESSIANIC PROPHECIES

The Old Testament Scriptures explicitly announce that He would be born of a virgin who would be overshadowed with the Holy Spirit.

150

nd she would bring forth a son, whose name would be "Wonderful," "Counsellor," "Everlasting God," "Mighty Father," "Prince of Peace." The New Testament Scriptures explain in detail the fulfillment of that prophecy. The angel Gabriel said the child to be born was the Son of God, and announced His name should be called Jesus, because He would save His people from their sins. At the baptismal waters, God said, "This is my beloved Son." John the Baptist said: "Behold the Lamb of God, that taketh away the sins of the world."

There are three hundred thirty-three distinct Messianic prophecies. These predict three hundred thirty-three things concerning the Christ, including His birth, the place in which He would be born, the manner of His birth, where He would reside as a child and grow up to manhood, His manner of life as a man, His miracles, His teaching, the place and manner of His death, the betrayal by one of His disciples, His burial in a borrowed tomb, the crucifixion of the thieves with Him, His resurrection from the dead, and His ascension to the Father. The three hundred thirty-three prophecies constitute the photograph of Him who was to come. When He came men looked on the one hand at the prophecies, or the photograph, on the other they saw the Man, and they said, "This is he of whom the prophets did write." He, and He only, fitted into every prophetic statement.

The Miracles of Christ

The miracles He wrought, His resurrection from the dead, His ascension to the Father, mark Him as the Son of God. If He were but a man and yet claimed to be the Christ, it is inconceivable that God would give Him miraculous power and raise Him from the dead. He proved to be true. He was honest in everything, therefore He spake the truth, and He declared Himself to be what the prophets had said He would be—the Son of God.

Being divine, Jesus Christ is our Saviour, Prophet, Priest and King. To Him hath all authority been given. His commands must be obeyed, His teaching accepted, His ordinances respected, and the church, which is His body, supported as the agency of His own adoption, to evangelize the world and to keep men in constant touch and fellowship with the heavenly Father. We say with the centurion who watched Him on the cross, "Surely this man is the Son of God."

CHRIST THE CREED

CHAPTER XXVIII

CHRIST THE CREED

When the Restoration movement began, the churches were under the oppression of human creeds, which were tests of fellowship. Alexander Campbell said in 1832: "By an authoritative human creed is meant an abstract of human opinions concerning the supposed cardinal articles of Christian faith, which summary is made a bond of union or term of communion."

The churches of Christ reject all such human authoritative creeds as tests of fellowship. It is perfectly proper to publish what one understands about the teaching of the Bible on any subject, as a matter of opinion. But to use such published statements as a condition of fellowship is unwarranted in the Scriptures. Isaac Errett published a tract called "Our Position." The writer of this book published a tract years ago entitled, "Facts Concerning the New Testament Church." These are not creeds—they are statements presented for information.

CHRIST THE CREED

In Matt. 16: 16 Peter said, "Thou art the Christ, the Son of the living God." That is known as the Good Confession. It is the acceptance of the Christ as the Son of God. Peter's statement does not constitute the creed. Christ Himself is the Creed. The word "creed" comes from *credo*—"I believe." We believe not in the statement about the Christ, but we believe in the Christ Himself. He is the foundation of the church. Paul said, "Other foundation can no man lay than that which is laid, which is Jesus Christ" (1 Cor. 3: 11). He is the creed that needs no revision. He is unchanging, the same yesterday, today and forever. He makes His appeal to all classes of people. He is adapted to the needs of men. He is understandable and furnishes a perfect model for imitation.

CONCERNING THE DISCIPLES

HUMAN CREEDS

All churches of Christendom which believe in the divinity of Christ accept Him as the Creed, but some are not satisfied to stop there. Many go beyond the Christ and present formulated statements of doctrine, which become confusing and serve to divide into many groups the believers in the Christ.

The great question that Jesus asked was this: "What think ye of the Christ? Whose son is he?" When a person comes forward, believing and penitent, to accept the Christ, he is not to be confronted with a group of abstract statements to which he must give assent. The Ethiopian who heard Philip preach Jesus, accepted Jesus as the Christ and was baptized into Him. When Paul preached to Lydia and her household there was a multitude of things with which they were not acquainted in the Christian system, but they accepted the center of that system—the Christ—and were baptized. On Pentecost, when Peter preached to the multitudes in Jerusalem, they heard him exalt the Christ, and, believing on the Christ, they said: "Men and brethren, what must we do?" And to that body of believers Peter said: "Repent and be baptized, every one of you, in the name of Jesus Christ, for the remission of your sins, and ye shall receive the gift of the Holy Spirit." Other items of Christian faith were to be learned as they progressed in the upward path, but the first essential was to believe in and accept the Christ.

If all human authoritative statements were abandoned and the believers in all Protestant bodies would unite upon the Christ and the simple steps required to enter into fellowship with Him, Christian union would come immediately. But it is the human creeds that constitute the dividing walls.

THE WEAKNESS OF HUMAN CREEDS

We are opposed to human creeds for the following reasons:

1. *Human creeds are not scriptural*. They are destitute of divine authority. There is no command in the Scripture to make them. They were not in use in New Testament times, during the first century of the church.

2. *They are too narrow*. They lay down a set of doctrines and

draw a circle around them, and only those who accept those doctrines are included; all others are excluded. Many earnest men who are inquirers after truth have been left out of the church because they could not accept the statements of men, yet were perfectly willing to accept Christ and His teachings. Those who do not accept the prescribed rules of a given body are frequently classed as heretics. The orthodox are those who are in agreement with the human creed of any given body.

3. *Human creeds overshadow the Christ.* We are commanded to hear Him (Matt. 17: 5); He is the head of the body—the church (Col. 1: 18), and, to Him hath been given all authority (Matt. 28: 18); He is the author and finisher of the faith (Heb. 12: 2); He must have pre-eminence (Col. 1: 18).

4. *Human creeds are insufficient.* They reflect the opinions of men, rather than the will of God. The interpretations of men are not always correct, as is seen by the variety of interpretations. Men who write the human creeds are not led by the Holy Spirit, for the Holy Spirit never contradicts. The Scriptures do not contradict, because they are written by "holy men of God who spake as they were moved by the Holy Spirit."

Christ is the head of the church. He has all authority, and He never delegated that authority to any man beyond the apostles, so, anything written other than that which has been expressly stated by the Christ and the apostles must not be accepted as binding upon the followers of Christ. Christ is the Creed and the Scriptures are the rule of faith and practice. On this position the churches of Christ have taken their stand. This position is impregnable, scriptural, and unifying.

THE NAME

CHAPTER XXIX

THE NAME

It must be remembered the churches of Christ make the plea for Christian unity through the restoration of the church of the New Testament. If it can be found that the New Testament church had a name, given by God, or the Christ, or the inspired apostles, we shall be on safe ground in applying that name to the people of God today. Our slogan is, "Where the Scriptures speak, we speak; and where the Scriptures are silent, we are silent." We shall, therefore, confine our investigation in this study to ascertaining the scriptural name.

Many human names are in vogue today, and all are divisive. Names are used to designate one party or group from the others. If there are many churches there will have to be many names. If there is one church one name will suffice. Names represent ideas, hence names have been selected for the various groups, signifying the things for which that group stands. If all the religious bodies were united, constituting the church as it was in the beginning, the differentiating names would disappear.

One of the things upon which churches must agree, before there can be organic union, is the name. Many of the names now in use are good and stand for great ideas, but any name other than the one used in the New Testament is narrow and divisive, and hence can not be selected as the name broad and inclusive enough for the united church.

Why should men busy themselves about naming an institution which has already been named? They can not improve upon the name given, therefore, why not be content with the name which has been assigned?

The Restoration movement seeks common ground upon which all can stand. Therefore, they must seek the name upon which all can agree. There is nothing sectarian or divisive in this.

CONCERNING THE DISCIPLES

THE NAME IN PROPHECY

The Old Testament has something to say about a name: Isa. 65: 15: "And ye shall leave your name for a curse unto my chosen; and the Lord Jehovah will slay thee; and he will call his servants by another *name*." Isa. 56: 5: "Unto them will I give in my house and within my walls a memorial and a *name* better than of sons and of daughters; I will give them an *everlasting name* that shall not be cut off." Isa. 62: 2: "And thou shalt be called by a *new name* which the mouth of Jehovah shall name." Amos 9: 11, 12: "In that day will I raise up the tabernacle of David that is fallen and close up the breaches thereof; and I will raise up its ruins, and I will build it as in the days of old; that they may possess the remnant of Edom; and all the nations that are called by *my name*, saith Jehovah that doeth this." These statements reveal that God would cast off the Jews and call His people by a *new name*, and the *name* would be a curse unto His "chosen." The name of Christ fulfills this prophecy. "The mouth of the Lord" bestowing this name means it will be given by inspiration. This name was to be better than the names of sons and daughters, meaning it would be better than all human names, and will be bestowed upon the children of God. John 1: 12, 13 and Rom. 8: 14-17 show that the followers of Christ are the children of God. These prophecies show that this is to be an everlasting name, and will be unchanging, and that it will be bestowed upon the Gentiles first, when God raises up the "tabernacle of David," which had fallen into ruins.

THE NAME GIVEN

In Acts 11: 26 we read: "The disciples were first called *Christians* at Antioch." This was the first Gentile church. In Acts 15: 14 we are told that God first visited Gentiles "to take out of them a people for *His name*." The prophecy of Amos 9: 11, 12, is quoted immediately following this statement, showing that the rebuilding of the "tabernacle of David" was a poetic reference to the establishment of the church. This name "Christian" was not given to the disciples at Antioch by way of derision, but it was spoken by "the mouth of the Lord," through inspiration.

162

THE NAME

HUMAN NAMES DIVISIVE

Human names did not come into existence, as applied to the disciples and the church, until centuries after the New Testament name was given. In Acts 26: 28 Agrippa was almost persuaded to become a *Christian*—not a Congregationalist, Episcopalian, or a Lutheran, for these names were unknown at that time. In 2 Pet. 4: 16, Peter says: "If any man suffer, let him suffer as a *Christian*"—not as a Lutheran, a Methodist or a Presbyterian, but "a *Christian*." In Phil. 2: 9-11 we read, God has given His Son a name which is "above every name." In 2 Cor. 11: 2 and Rev. 21: 2, Christ is the bridegroom, and the bride, which is the church, should wear the name of the bridegroom. In Eph. 3: 14, 15, the church of Christ is presented as God's family, and "*Christian*" is the family name. In Acts 4: 12, we are told there is salvation in no other *name*, hence we should wear the *name of Christ*. In Matt. 28: 19 and Acts 2: 39, we learn that when men are baptized the name of Christ is called upon them. At this time we assume the divine name, with its obligations. We are baptized in the name of Jesus Christ. According to Rev. 22: 3, 4, this name will be upon our foreheads hereafter, making it an everlasting name that shall not be cut off.

IMPORTANCE OF THE NAME

There is something in a name. If you don't believe it, sign some other man's name to your check and present it to the bank. If there is nothing in a name, why are you particular about the name of the proper person being signed to the check that is handed you? If there is nothing in a name, you would be as happy to be called a liar as an honest man. Names stand for something, and a man is very particular as to what he may be called.

In our relation one to another we are *brethren*. As students of the great *Teacher* we are *disciples*. When it comes to perfection of character, of being set apart to Christian work, the Bible knows the followers of Christ as *saints*. When the broad term is used covering the sons and daughters of God—disciples of Christ, the word "*Christian*" was given; and the body of believers as a whole, constituting the church, is known as the *church of Christ* (Rom. 16: 16).

163

WHAT MUST I DO TO BE SAVED?

CHAPTER XX.

WHAT MUST I DO TO BE SAVED?

God teaches us through the Scriptures that man is lost and can be saved: "All have sinned and come short of the glory of God." "Whosoever calleth on the name of the Lord shall be saved." "It is the Father's good pleasure that not one should perish." Jesus said, "I came to seek and to save that which is lost."

Two Sides to Salvation

There are two sides to a man's salvation—the divine and the human. From the time of man's transgression in the Garden of Eden until the establishing of the church on Pentecost, the processes were at work for the redemption of humanity.

On the divine side are God, the Father; Jesus Christ, the Saviour, who made the atonement with His death upon the cross; and the Scriptures, revealing the plan of God. This can be summed up in the words, "grace" and "mercy." On the human side man is active in his own salvation. He must accept and appropriate that which is offered. He must hear the Word, and hearing produces faith. Being convinced of sin and having godly sorrow for sin, he is led to repentance. Believing in and unashamed of the Christ, he will confess Him. Then the penitent becomes willing to meet his Lord where the Lord has promised to meet him. He symbolizes his Lord's death, burial and resurrection in the act of Christian baptism, which is loving obedience to his Lord's command. In this act he puts on Jesus Christ. "For as many as has been baptized into Christ did put on Christ."

The Divine Plan

This is the divine plan of human redemption. It is fully and simply expressed in the New Testament Scriptures. Before returning to the Father, Jesus gave the marching orders to His church, found in Mark 16: 16: "Go ye into all the world and preach the gospel to every creature. He that believeth and is baptized shall be saved, and he that believeth not shall be condemned."

The disciples were told to tarry in Jerusalem until endued with power from on high. They were told when the Spirit of truth would come He would guide them into all truth. They tarried and the Spirit of truth came, and on Pentecost, having declared the Lordship of Jesus, Peter said to the inquiring, believing multitude, "Repent and be baptized, every one of you, in the name of Jesus Christ, for the remission of sins, and ye shall receive the gift of the Holy Spirit." That proclaimed by Peter in answer to the inquirers after salvation, was in direct harmony with the Great Commission, given by Jesus before the ascension.

THE APOSTOLIC PRACTICE

The Acts of the Apostles contains the record of apostolic evangelism. Men preached, being moved by the Holy Spirit. That record of evangelism harmonizes with the Great Commission. That plan has never changed. The Christ, who had all authority, has never delegated authority to any individual to change His plan and purpose. That plan was given for the Christian dispensation, which will last until the coming of the Lord. So the laws of the Lord concerning redemption are in force today.

Before the death of Jesus He could save any man in any way He saw fit, for His will had not gone into effect. On the day of Pentecost His will, as expressed in the Great Commission, went into effect, and from that day on men are saved when they comply with the conditions stipulated in that will. In the days of His personal ministry, Jesus could say to one, "Leave all and follow me"; to another, "This day thou shalt be with me in paradise." But His executors must present the will as written and point men to compliance with that will, in order that divine favor of forgiveness may be granted. Therefore, we ask the question, "What must an unbeliever do to be saved?" We take him right where he is. Naturally, the first step is to produce faith, to make him a believer. In Acts, sixteenth chapter, we find such an individual in the person of the

Philippian jailer. Paul said to him, "Believe on the Lord Jesus Christ." We learn, after having been taught by Paul so that he did become a believer, he was baptized the same hour.

What must a believer do to be saved? People in Jerusalem, on the Day of Pentecost, having heard the preaching, were led to believe, and when they asked what to do were told to repent and be baptized (Acts 2: 38).

What shall a penitent believer do? The answer is found in the case of Saul of Tarsus (Acts 9 and 22). He was told to go into Damascus, and there it would be told him what to do. Ananias was sent by the Lord to Paul and told that penitent believer to "arise and be baptized and wash away thy sins, calling on the name of the Lord."

What shall a baptized, penitent believer do to be saved, when he has backslidden? The answer is found in Acts, eighth chapter, in the case of Simon. Peter said to him, "Repent and pray God that the thought of thine heart may be forgiven thee."

God's plan of salvation is rational, simple, and understandable. It meets the need of man, and when complied with is satisfactory to all. If we do what the Lord commands us to do we have faith to believe that He will do what He has promised to do.

ONLY ONE PLAN

This plan fits in beautifully with the Great Commission, with Christ's teaching to Nicodemus concerning the new birth, and with the New Testament teaching of a change of heart. It is the uniform plan proclaimed in the Scriptures. There has been since the creation of man one law of physical birth. It is reasonable to believe that God, who gave the law of physical birth, would also in this Christian dispensation, have only one law for the spiritual birth. That law is found in the New Testament.

BAPTISM—ITS IMPORTANCE

CHAPTER XXXI

BAPTISM—ITS IMPORTANCE

The churches of Christ believe in and are followers of the Christ. They observe the ordinances of Christ because He ordained them. This explains their adherence to the ordinance of Christian baptism, and of the Lord's Supper.

So far as baptism is concerned, they are a misunderstood people. Some believe they worship the ordinance. They have been accused of believing in baptismal regeneration—water salvation. Some have accused them of teaching that all a man needs to do to be saved is to be baptized. In none of these accusations is there any truth. This and the following chapters on the subject of baptism are intended to set squarely before the people their position on the baptismal question.

Baptism has back of it the authority of Jesus Christ, or it does not have His authority. It is important or it is unimportant. In this chapter we are considering the authority and the importance of baptism.

JOHN HONORED BAPTISM

John the Baptist derived his name, "Baptist," from the fact he was the baptizer. He was sent of God, and the work he did was ordained of God. He preached the baptism of repentance and baptized many in the Jordan and at Enon, near Salem.

CHRIST HONORED BAPTISM

Christ honored baptism. He traveled between sixty and seventy miles to be baptized by John in Jordan, and said, "Thus it becometh us to fulfil all righteousness" (Matt. 3: 15). He placed it in the Great Commission, saying, "Go ye into all the world and preach the gospel to every creature; he that believeth and is baptized shall be saved." In this commission He joined preaching and baptism. Nothing should be declared unimportant which is found in the Great Commission.

GOD HONORED BAPTISM

God honored the institution by acknowledging Christ to be His Son, at the time He was baptized, saying, "This is my beloved Son, in whom I am well pleased" (Matt. 3: 17).

THE APOSTLES HONORED BAPTISM

The apostles honored baptism, commanding it in every case where people believed on the Christ and were added to the church.

On Pentecost, Peter said to the inquiring Jews, "Repent and be baptized, every one of you, in the name of Jesus Christ, for the remission of sins, and ye shall receive the gift of the Holy Spirit" (Acts 2: 38).

Philip presented the subject of baptism to the Ethiopian eunuch, for, having heard him preach, the eunuch said, "See, here is water; what doth hinder me to be baptized?" And Philip and the eunuch both went down into the water, and he baptized him. (Acts 8: 36-38).

Ananias said to Saul of Tarsus, "And now why tarriest thou? Arise and be baptized and wash away thy sins, calling on the name of the Lord" (Acts 22: 16).

Peter having preached to the household of Cornelius, and seeing the Holy Spirit falling upon that group, giving proof that they were to be recipients of the gospel, as well as the Jews, turned to the Jews who had accompanied him from Joppa, and said: "Can any man forbid water that these should not be baptized which have received the Holy Spirit as well as we? And he commanded them to be baptized in the name of the Lord" (Acts 10: 47, 48).

Paul said something about baptism to Lydia and her household, for "she attended unto the things which were spoken of Paul, and when she was baptized and her household, she besought us saying, if ye have judged me to be faithful to the Lord, come unto my house and abide there" (Acts 16: 15).

Paul preached baptism to the jailer and his household, for they were baptized the same hour of the night (Acts 16: 33).

BAPTISM—ITS IMPORTANCE

Paul preached baptism to the Corinthians, for we read, "Many of the Corinthians hearing, believed and were baptized" (Acts 18: 18).

Baptism was preached by Paul at Ephesus, for we read: "And when they heard this they were baptized in the name of the Lord Jesus" (Acts 19: 5).

Baptism was preached to the Romans, for Paul said: "Are ye ignorant that all we who were baptized into Jesus Christ were baptized into his death?" (Rom. 6: 3).

It was preached to the Galatians, for Paul said: "As many of you as were baptized into Christ did put on Christ" (Gal. 3: 27).

It was preached to the Colossians, for Paul said of them, "Having been buried with him in baptism, ye were also raised with him through faith in the workings of God, who raised him from the dead" (Col. 2: 12).

Peter refers to it in 1 Pet. 3: 21, in referring to the eight souls saved in the ark: "A like figure whereunto even baptism doth also now save us."

BAPTISM IS ASSOCIATED WITH SALVATION

Baptism is associated with salvation: "He that believeth and is baptized shall be saved."

It is declared to be the ordinance by which we get into Christ—His body, the church. "Know ye not that so many of us as were baptized into Jesus Christ were baptized into his death" (Rom. 6: 3).

Baptism is symbolic, symbolizing the death, the burial, and the resurrection of Jesus Christ from the dead. (Rom. 6: 4, 5).

From the above it is clearly seen that baptism is not of man's making or choosing. It has been given by Him who has "all authority." If we accept Christ we must accept His ordinances. In preaching the gospel we declare the death, burial and resurrection of Christ, and baptism is interwoven symbolically with those events.

BAPTISM—THE ACTION

CHAPTER XXXII

BAPTISM—THE ACTION

The law of baptism is given by Christ in the Great Commission (Matt. 28: 18-20). During the first century, while the apostles, guided by the Holy Spirit, were preaching, there was no question concerning the action of baptism. Christ was immersed, and all who came into the church from Pentecost on were immersed.

THE MEANING OF THE WORD

The word *"baptizo"* means to immerse, to plunge, to dip. It is a well understood fact that the primary interpretation of all writings, sacred and profane, is to give words the meaning which they have in their historic sense. Language is used to communicate ideas, and words must be taken in the sense in which those who employ them know they will be understood. It is a matter of law that when a law is uncertain there is no law. If the question of baptism, therefore, be uncertain, no baptism is required. But, the word "baptism" has one meaning and is easily understood, and is binding through the Christian dispensation.

Today the ordinance is performed in one of three ways—by immersion, pouring, or sprinkling. There is only one baptism, therefore only one of these can be right. The word referring to baptism in the New Testament is the Greek word *baptizo*, which is always translated "to dip, or to immerse." The Greek word for the specific act of pouring is *cheo;* and the Greek word for sprinkling in *raino,* and the word using water, regardless of the manner, is *hudraino.* These last three words are never used in connection with baptism. If Jesus had meant that people should be sprinkled, *raino* would be used; if pouring, *cheo;* if the form made no difference, then *hudraino.* All great Greek scholars, ancient and modern, are in complete accord in this matter.

179

CONCERNING THE DISCIPLES

The Circumstantial Evidence

The circumstantial evidence furnished by the Scriptures themselves is one hundred per cent for immersion. John was baptizing at Enon, near Salem, because there was much water, or, many water (John 3: 23). They went to the water (Acts 8: 39). They went down into the water (Acts 8: 38). They came up out of the water (Matt. 3: 6; Acts 8: 39). Baptism is a form of birth (John 3: 5) and a form of resurrection (Rom. 6: 4); a form of burial (Col. 2: 12); a form of planting [covered up] (Rom. 6: 5); a washing of the whole body (Heb. 10: 22). Note always that an immersion requires water, much water, going to the water, going into the water, coming out of the water. It presents a picture of birth, burial, resurrection, planting, and has the body washed, whereas sprinkling and pouring simply require water, and only a little of it. Baptism is a symbol of the death, burial, and resurrection of the Christ. The symbol is destroyed in sprinkling or in pouring.

Nowhere in either the Old or the New Testament is there any reference to water alone ever being sprinkled on anybody. Clean water is referred to in Ezek. 36: 25, but the Book of Numbers, chapter 19, explains that clean water is the water of purification, the water of separation, and is water mixed with the ashes of a heifer, which makes lye, and is applied to the person for a legal cleansing. In all cases where the word "sprinkling" is used, it refers either to the sprinkling of blood, blood and oil, blood and water, or ashes and water, and in none of these cases is the thought of Christian baptism presented.

Christian baptism belongs to the Christian dispensation, and went into force on the day of Pentecost, the day the church was instituted.

Why "Baptizo" Was Not Translated

When the Bishops' Bible was translated, in 1561, the doctrine of John Calvin, the substitution of sprinkling for immersion, was being agitated. To prevent controversy the word *"baptizo"* was not translated, but was Anglicized, which means, carrying over the pronunciation without translating the word; so, the Greek word *baptizo*, instead of being translated immerse, retained its original form, in part, by dropping its last letter and substituting the letter "e." If John

180

alvin had not been agitating sprinkling as a substitute for immersion
he word here would have been translated, as it was in the Old Testament, in 2 Kings 5: 10-14, where Naaman dipped in the Jordan seven
imes. In the Hebrew that word is *tabhal*; in the Greek, *baptizo*, and
translated in the English, "dip." If *baptizo* is translated "dip" in the
Old Testament, it should also be translated "dip" in the New Testament. But again we state, it was not translated at all, but was merely
Anglicized. When the King James translation was made in 1611, the
word *baptizo* again was Anglicized, the same as it had been in the
Bishops' Bible, for at this time there still was an effort to substitute
sprinkling for immersion. Other translations having followed this
custom, explains our having *baptizo* untranslated.

How Sprinkling Originated

The first case of affusion, so far as history records, was in A. D.
51, when Novotian desired to be baptized while on a sick bed.
Being unable to be taken to the water, they poured water around
im until his body was covered. Note, that was in the third century.

The first law of sprinkling was obtained in 753, from Pope Stephen
I, who permitted pouring and sprinkling in cases of necessity.

In 1311, the Legislature, in Council at Ravenna, declared immersion
or sprinkling to be indifferent.

At the Council of Constans, about 1356, a decree was made legal-
zing all such cases of clinic or sickly baptism already past or that
might come in the future.

The Anglican Church, which sprang from the Roman Catholic,
began in 1534; the Presbyterian, an offshoot from the Anglican, began
about 1541; and the Congregational Church soon after. It is a historic fact that for about one hundred years these churches practiced
immersion. The Westminster Assembly was called together by the
Parliament of England in 1643, and voted to substitute sprinkling for
immersion. It was a tie vote, which led Dr. Lightfoot, the president
of the Assembly, to cast the deciding vote, which favored the substitution.

In 1664, the Parliament of England repealed that part of the
old law which enforced immersion, and passed a new law, enforcing
sprinkling in its stead. This change came long after the Scriptures

were written. Christ and the apostles had nothing to do with it. Sprinkling as a substitute for immersion owes its origin today to Roman Catholicism, John Calvin, the Westminster Assembly of 1643 and to the Parliament of England, in 1644.

UNIVERSALLY ACCEPTED BAPTISM

The churches of Christ, desiring to restore the church of the New Testament, stand on the plain New Testament ground when they go back of all legislation to practice the ordinance which symbolizes the death, the burial, and the resurrection of the Christ. This is universal baptism. While some contend that sprinkling or pouring may do as well, all agree that immersion measures up to the baptism of the New Testament. No one immersed ever desires to be sprinkled while many who are sprinkled are later immersed. Substitute the words "sprinkle" or "pour" in every case in the New Testament where baptism is recorded, and in nearly every case the sense is incomplete. Substitute immerse for the word "baptize," and in every case, without a single exception, the sense is complete. The religious world will never unite on sprinkling or pouring as baptism, but all do acknowledge that immersion is the New Testament action, therefore it becomes the unifying action for all.

To be convinced study the New Testament with an unbiased mind. The baptismal question has been treated too lightly. The open Book studied with an open mind makes the way clear.

BAPTISM—THE DESIGN

CHAPTER XXXIII

BAPTISM—THE DESIGN

The importance of baptism is shown in its design. It is not an idle command. The command is positive. The fact that baptism is a part of the Great Commission and is associated with all cases of conversion recorded in the Acts of the Apostles and in references to conversion in the Epistles, mark it as being of importance.

Baptism is associated with the authority of Christ, with the preaching of the gospel, with belief, with repentance, with confession, with forgiveness of sins, with the Holy Spirit, with the new creature, with the spiritual birth, with salvation, with the death, burial and resurrection of Christ, with the putting on of Christ, with the new life, and with the body of Christ—the church.

BAPTISM IS INTRODUCTORY

Baptism brings the penitent believer into the proper relationship to the Father, Son and Holy Spirit. "Go teach all nations, baptizing them into the name of the Father, Son and Holy Spirit" (Matt. 28: 18). "Except a man be born of water and of the Spirit he cannot enter into the kingdom of God" (John 3: 5). "Are ye ignorant that all we who were baptized into the Lord Jesus Christ were baptized into his death?" (Rom. 6: 3). "For in one spirit we were all baptized into one body" (1 Cor. 12: 13). The body of Christ is His church. "For as many of you as were baptized into Christ have put on Christ" (Gal. 3: 27). The Scriptures teach we are brought into this new relationship by baptism.

BAPTISM IS FOR THE REMISSION OF SINS

The meritorious cause of pardon is in the blood of Jesus Christ. "Christ died for our sins." "Much more then, being now justified by

13

his blood, we shall be saved from the wrath of God through him." "In whom we have our redemption through his blood." "Unto him that loved us and loosed us from our sins by his blood." The merit lies in the blood of Christ. Baptism is a condition upon which the forgiveness of sins is obtained. Through baptism we appropriate the death of Christ unto ourselves. It is the place appointed of God to meet the sinner who through faith and repentance comes to this obedience and is granted the forgiveness of his sins. The blood of Christ is the ground of pardon. Baptism is the expression and condition of our acceptance of that pardon.

To show that baptism has a place in the remission of sins, note these Scriptures: "He that believeth and is baptized shall be saved" (Mark 16: 16). Peter said on Pentecost, "Repent ye and be baptized, every one of you, in the name of Jesus Christ, unto the remission of your sins, and ye shall receive the gift of the Holy Spirit" (Acts 2: 38). This is in accord with the Great Commission. To Saul, Ananias said, "Arise and be baptized and wash away thy sins, calling on his name" (Acts 22: 16). "If any man be in Christ he is a new creature: old things are passed away; behold, all things are become new" (2 Cor. 5: 17). "In whom we have redemption through his blood, even the forgiveness of sins" (Col. 1: 14; Gal. 1: 7). Baptism is called a birth (John 3: 5). We are born into the kingdom by the birth of water and of spirit; a newborn babe is sinless, so newborn babes in Christ being freed from sin and having received pardon from God, stand sinless before Him.

Baptism Is a Symbol

Some claim, "baptism is just a form." It is more than a form, but if it be a form, it must be a form of something. The action bespeaks the form. It is the symbol of death, burial, resurrection and a birth. The symbol can only be expressed in preserving the proper form. Immersion meets that requirement.

The Promise of the Holy Spirit

The baptized believer is a new creature in Christ and belongs to Christ's body—the church. His faith, repentance, confession and

186

baptism have placed him there, and he now is to be the recipient of the Holy Spirit, and his life will manifest forth the fruits of the Spirit, if he abide in Christ and Christ's Word abides in him. The Holy Spirit is not promised to the world, but to Christians, and the last step one takes in becoming a Christian is the obedience in Christian baptism.

187

BAPTISM—THE PROPER SUBJECTS

CHAPTER XXXIV

BAPTISM—THE PROPER SUBJECTS

Baptism is introductory for the remission of sins, and is symbolical of the death, burial and resurrection of Christ. The antecedents of baptism are: hearing, faith, repentance and confession. To need baptism one must have sins to be remitted. The antecedents and consequence of Christian baptism make it impossible for it to apply to infants.

PENITENT BELIEVERS FIT SUBJECTS

Jesus said (Mark 16: 16): "He that believeth and is baptized shall be saved." Infants can not believe. Peter said (Acts 2: 38), "Repent and be baptized, every one of you, in the name of Jesus Christ, for the remission of sins." Infants can not repent, nor do they have need of repentance. They have no sins to be remitted, hence baptism does not apply to them.

Peter said, "Baptism is not a putting away of the filth of the flesh," such as taking a bath, washing the body, "but," he said, "it is the answer of a good conscience toward God." A little infant does not have any conscience, hence can not know when he is obeying God.

INFANT BAPTISM UNSCRIPTURAL

There is no precept or example in the New Testament for infant baptism. In all four of the household baptisms, found in Acts, tenth chapter, sixteenth chapter and 1 Corinthians, sixteenth chapter, it is clearly shown that there were conditions there to be observed which in no case could apply to infants. In those household baptisms the baptized were hearers, believers, penitent, they rejoiced, and they served, none of which can apply to an infant.

Baptism is for the remission of sins which one commits. Infants do not commit sin. Baptism is not for the sin of Adam, for Adam's sin is punished by physical death and is visited on the entire race of men. "As in Adam all die, so in Christ shall all be made alive."

Infant baptism began in the third century, a long time after the last line of Scripture had been written. There is no item of teaching relative to infant baptism found in the Scriptures.

Churches practicing infant baptism sprinkle infants on the ground that they have sin, which must be remitted by baptism. If that were the case, the infant having no faith, no repentance, no confession, would be receiving baptismal regeneration, against which the churches which practice it openly rebel.

Some claim that parents have the babies sprinkled that in the act they may take a vow to rear them correctly. If that be true, is it not strange that many are never concerned about baptizing the babe until they think he is going to die? Then they send for a preacher at the midnight hour to hurry and baptize the baby. If they know the baby is going to die, is there any need of taking a vow to rear it aright? One does not take a vow to provide for the material needs of the child, why the necessity of such a vow for the spiritual needs? Furthermore, the Scriptures nowhere authorize that any such vow be taken, or, if taken, that it be associated with baptism, for baptism is to bring a blessing to the recipient, and not to the sponsors of the same. Baptism is performed by the authority of Jesus Christ, and Christ gave no authority for people to take this ordinance and make it an oath or a vow that they will do their duty toward their offspring.

Some argue that baptism takes the place of circumcision. The position can not be substantiated in Scripture. Circumcision was practiced to show the fleshly relation of the babe to the theocratic government, while baptism is the act by which one puts on Jesus Christ. In circumcision only the males were circumcised, whereas in infant baptism both males and females are sprinkled. If baptism takes the place of circumcision, it will apply to males only, and if it be for the forgiveness of sins, then the females would not have their sins remitted. The males were circumcised when eight days old, whereas infant baptism takes place any time during infancy. Christ was circumcised at the age of eight days. He was also baptized at the age of thirty years, when He began His ministry. All the men who joined the church at Jerusalem on the day of Pentecost had been circumcised. They were also on that day baptized. If baptism takes the place of circumcision, why were those circumcised Jews under the necessity of being baptized?

Some maintain that the statement, "Suffer the little children to come unto me" refers to baptism. There is no allusion here to baptism. That statement was made before Christian baptism was instituted. Jesus simply expressed the desire to have little children come to Him. When He said, "Of such is the kingdom of heaven" He was conveying the same thought expressed when He said, "Except ye be converted and become as a little child ye shall not enter into the kingdom of heaven." He was not discussing church membership, forgiveness of sins, nor baptism, in this connection.

The harm of infant baptism is shown in the fact that the administrator in sprinkling water upon a babe says, "By the authority of Jesus Christ I baptize you." He hasn't any authority from Jesus Christ to do that. When an infant is baptized he is robbed of that part of his experimental religion. Baptism is an experience, but a baby does not have it.

Baptism is a voluntary act, accepted by the penitent believer, whereas in infant baptism the infant is forced to submit to the substitute ordinance.

Christ died for the babies as well as for the adults. When one has come to the age of accountability he is commanded to render obedience and to appropriate Christ's death for his salvation. Until that time has been reached the child remains in a state of innocence, and his state of salvation is already assured without his having to appropriate the shedding of blood in his behalf. That appropriation comes when he is able to hear, to believe, to repent, and to be baptized.

Paul said (Rom. 6: 18), in referring to baptism, "Ye have obeyed from the heart that form of doctrine." The form of doctrine is here shown in the early part of the chapter, when he refers to baptism as being a burial and a resurrection. The Romans who thus rendered obedience knew what they were doing, for they obeyed from the heart the form of doctrine—the form of baptism—the immersion in water.

There is not one line of Scripture from which one can even take the inference that infants are to be baptized.

THE LORD'S SUPPER

CHAPTER XXXV

THE LORD'S SUPPER

Jesus said, "I am the living bread which came down from heaven: if any man eat of this bread he shall live for ever; and the bread that I will give is my flesh, which I will give for the life of the world. The Jews, therefore, strove among themselves, saying, How can this man give us his flesh to eat? Then Jesus said unto them, Verily, verily, I say unto you, except ye eat the flesh of the Son of man, and drink his blood, ye have no life in you. Whoso eateth my flesh and drinketh my blood, hath eternal life: and I will raise him up at the last day" (John 6: 51-54).

Its Importance

Even the disciples of Jesus said, "This is a hard saying: who can hear it?" He was here speaking metaphorically. The full explanation is made later when the Lord's Supper was instituted, for in Matt. 26: 26-28 we read: "And as they were eating Jesus took bread and blessed it and brake it and gave it to the disciples and said, Take, eat; this is my body. And he took the cup, and gave thanks and gave it to them, saying, Drink ye all of it; for this is my blood of the New Testament, which is shed for many for the remission of sins." The disciples now saw that the bread and the wine represented the flesh and blood. These Scriptures explain the importance of the Lord's Supper. In observing it we acknowledge Christ as the source of our spiritual life.

It is a memorial, given by the Christ to commemorate His death and to show forth that death until He come (1 Cor. 11: 26).

Who May Commune?

Who has a right to sit at the Lord's Table? To whom has the Lord given the institution? It is for every believer in the Christ, for those who are citizens of His kingdom, and who desire to remember His death and show forth His coming. The Lord's Supper is spiritual food for the spiritual man, and before the spiritual man can observe the ordinance and partake of the food he must be born. This would exclude those who are aliens to Christ, men who remain in their sins, who are not born into the kingdom of God.

In observing the Lord's Supper we commune with Christ, and not with men. This puts to flight the doctrine of "close communion," so called. The closeness of it is shown in the individual communing with his Christ. Each individual partakes of the loaf and of the cup, and in so doing he remembers the Christ and he also shows forth His death until He come. Jesus said, "Do this in remembrance of me." Paul said, "The cup of blessing which we bless, is it not the communion of the blood of Christ? The bread which we break, is it not the communion of the body of Christ?" (1 Cor. 10: 16). This makes it personal, individual.

Frequency of Its Observance

How often shall one commune? Every institution has a set time for its observance. The Passover, the covenant feast of Israel, was kept on the fourteenth day of Abib, or Nisan (Ex. 12: 3, 6, 17). The feast of weeks, or Pentecost, was held at a given time every year (Lev. 23: 15, 16). All institutions of God had a definite time for their observance. When Jesus said, "Do this in remembrance of me," He would undoubtedly have set a time for that remembrance. We read (Acts 20: 7), "And upon the first day of the week, when the disciples came together to break bread, Paul preached unto them." This does not mean they came together upon the first day of some week, but they came together upon the first day of *the* week, which can be interpreted only as meaning the first day, or the Lord's Day of every week. The shewbread, which was the type of Christ, was renewed every week in the old dispensation. "And thou shalt take fine flour and bake twelve cakes thereof; two-tenth deals shall be in one cake. *Every sabbath* he shall set it in order before the Lord continually, being taken from the children of Israel by the everlasting covenant" (Lev. 24: 5, 8). "And other of the brethren, of the sons of Kohathites, were over the shewbread to prepare it every sabbath" (1 Chron. 9: 32). The shewbread, the type of Christ, being renewed once a week, would indicate that the bread and wine, representing the flesh and blood, should also be renewed each week in the new dispensation. And that is exactly what happened, as is explained by the weekly observance in the New Testament.

NATURE OF ITS OBSERVANCE

Paul has given instructions in 1 Cor. 11: 20-34 as to the proper observance of the institution. The Corinthians did not discern the Lord's body, but brought their baskets and ate their meals, thinking of feeding the body, rather than remembering the Christ. The Lord's Supper is not a time to feast the body, but the spirit. We eat not to satisfy material hunger, but spiritual. One should be meditative, thoughtful and reverent in the observance. This worship will carry us back to the sacrifice that was made in our behalf, and will point forward to the return of the Lord. It is a memory and a hope, a looking back and a looking forward. The Lord's Supper is a means to an end. It is to help the memory; it is to deepen the spiritual life and awaken within us the expectancy of His coming.

THE FUTURE OF THE MOVEMENT

CHAPTER XXXVI

THE FUTURE OF THE MOVEMENT

We have come a long way in one hundred twenty-five years. The Restoration movement originated on American soil. From a score of individuals it has grown to number within our brotherhood one and a half million strong, to say nothing of the influence which has been exerted among the religious bodies of the United States. We have a glorious past. The question now before us is, what of the future? The goal has not been reached. Our plea is the unity of all followers of Christ. While there is a finer feeling among all religious bodies, Christian unity does not yet obtain in full measure. We still have a long way to go before the prayer of our Lord for the unity of believers will be answered.

CONVICTION NECESSARY

We believe we have been called to the kingdom for such a time as this. People are rapidly losing interest in denominationalism and are coming to take their stand against these unnecessary divisions. Many are in the dark and are looking for a Moses to lead them out. The only sane basis for the desired union is to be found in the New Testament Scriptures. Knowing that basis as we do, it is incumbent upon our folk to make it known to the religious world.

Because of the friendliness that exists among religious bodies, there is too frequently a tendency to give but little stress to the things that have given us existence and made us a strong people.

INDOCTRINATION NECESSARY

The success of the future demands that we indoctrinate our own people. There are too many in the Christian church everywhere unacquainted with our history, and the pioneers who did the pioneering of other days, and the doctrines that are paramount in the Word of God. The essential doctrines must be taught in the Bible school, discussed in young people's societies, presented in sermon, and studied in the quietness of the family circle. It still remains true that people "do err, not knowing the scriptures."

PROCLAMATION NECESSARY

The denominational world does not know us. One of our preachers inquired of a postmaster in a village in a Western city thirty years ago as to what churches were in the village. Being told, he asked, "For what does the Presbyterian Church stand?" The answer came speedily, "To make people better—prepare them for heaven." He then asked, "For what does the Methodist Church stand?" The reply was, "For the same thing the Presbyterian Church does." The inquirer then said, "For what does the Christian Church stand?" And immediately the postmaster replied, "Baptism." Probably the majority of the postmasters, as well as the other people of the towns and the villages throughout our land, would give the same answer. We are not Baptists; we do not follow an ordinance nor name ourselves after the ordinance. Our faith does not center in baptism. We believe in Jesus Christ and are baptized because He commanded it. Some not knowing our position, have accused us falsely of being narrow, of having monopolized the word "Christian," of not believing in prayer, and having no regard for the Holy Spirit. All of these accusations are unjust. To eradicate this criticism we must teach and preach "in season and out of season."

Well written doctrinal tracts should be distributed by the membership of the churches to every individual in the community where the church stands. If the proper literature could be placed in the hands of every denominational preacher in America wonders would be worked among the churches in the next ten months. The story of the pioneers and their work should be found in the home of every disciple of Christ. It furnishes "truth that is stranger than fiction." Nothing so fascinating is being written in these days.

Bible study is one of the needs of the hour. Knowledge is received by teaching—"here a little and there a little, line upon line, and precept upon precept."

THE FUTURE OF THE MOVEMENT

A new day is dawning. People will ultimately join the parade ading back to the church. A people with nothing to preach but he gospel, and nothing to do but preach the gospel, should be ready, ith lantern in hand, to guide the returning forces through the dark-ess to the light.

Our church papers should be in the homes of all our people. The ooks and tracts that deal with the essential things of the gospel hould be on every table and on the shelves of our libraries. An nformed people can give information.

RIGHTEOUS LIVING NECESSARY

It remains true that "a tree is known by its fruits." Of all peo-les in the world the disciples of Christ should live the best lives, e the most united, most aggressive, most optimistic, and should be nost active in the evangelistic program to win the men of the world. A people with so great a plea must live a correspondingly great life. This done, the world will see our good works and glorify our Father n heaven.

9741